"There is no one I know who can stir the hearts of leaders, especially those who are emerging and younger leaders, as Daniel Allen. I have been privileged to have a front row seat to see it occur. As you read *Summoned* you will be challenged to not stay where you are as a leader. Be prepared to encounter the grand narrative of King Jesus, and the unique story he is writing into the hearts and lives of those of us who follow him. May each of us respond in new fresh ways to his summons on our lives. I highly recommend this new work!"

**Terry Walling,** president, Leader Breakthru

"Daniel Allen shares real life experiences and the insights that he's gained to help us travel on a clear path toward discovering God's dreams and designs for our lives. This book is so important because we can too easily find ourselves misaligned and in pursuit of our own dreams and striving to design our own lives instead of aligning ourselves with God's."

**Steve Saccone,** author of *Protege: Developing Your Next Generation of Leaders*

"What does it mean—really—to follow God? How does God's call impact our jobs, our relationships, our thoughts? With warmth and candor, Daniel Allen provides clear direction for every young person who wants to know how their life matters to the world. Perfect as a resource for a mentoring relationship or as a gift to a young leader, *Summoned* speaks into today's culture with accuracy, strength and hope. I'll be keeping multiple copies on hand—and anyone who has a desire to see the best out of young leaders will want to as well."

**Nicole Unice,** ministry leader at Hope Church in Richmond, Virginia, and author of *Start Here* and *She's Got Issues*

D1510727

"The difference between leaders and followers is perspective. The difference between leaders and better leaders is better perspective. Daniel Allen's book, *Summoned,* is about giving leaders a heads-up on better perspectives they will need all during their lives and ministry. The strength of the book lies in the many personal illustrations, both from his own life and from folks he has personally observed, which underlie excellent guidelines and principles. These personal anecdotes authenticate his experiential learned guidelines and principles. Forewarned is forearmed. Daniel's book will do just that. Leader, read it and get better perspective on many leadership issues."

**J. Robert Clinton,** retired professor of leadership, School of InterCultural Studies, Fuller Theological Seminary

"In *Summoned,* Daniel Allen provides a compelling invitation to follow Jesus with our whole lives. With deep and accessible wisdom, he addresses common issues faced by American men in the journey of discipleship. He does not remain fixated on issues and barriers, but he calls us to profound transformation and flourishing leadership. I recommend this book especially to men in their twenties and thirties."

**Jason Jensen,** national field director and Discipleship Steering Committee chair, InterVarsity Christian Fellowship

"Throughout over twenty-five years of pastoral ministry, hands down, the most frequently asked question I have been posed has to do with knowing God's will in relation to personal calling. In this book Daniel Allen has given us all a gift. I just wish I would have had it throughout the years to hand to others. *Summoned* is a treasure box of wisdom and encouragement."

**Lance Ford,** author of *UnLeader* and *Revangelical*

# SUMMONED

## STEPPING UP TO LIVE AND
## LEAD WITH JESUS

## DANIEL ALLEN JR.

### Foreword by HUGH HALTER

IVP Books

An imprint of InterVarsity Press
Downers Grove, Illinois

InterVarsity Press
P.O. Box 1400, Downers Grove, IL 60515-1426
ivpress.com
email@ivpress.com

InterVarsity Press® is the book-publishing division of InterVarsity Christian Fellowship/USA®, a
movement of students and faculty active on campus at hundreds of universities, colleges and schools
of nursing in the United States of America, and a member movement of the International Fellowship
of Evangelical Students. For information about local and regional activities, visit intervarsity.org.

All Scripture quotations, unless otherwise indicated, are taken from THE HOLY BIBLE, NEW
INTERNATIONAL VERSION®, NIV® Copyright © 1973, 1978, 1984, 2011 by Biblica, Inc.™ Used by
permission. All rights reserved worldwide.

Published in association with the literary agency of WordServe Literary Group, Ltd., www.
wordserveliterary.com.

While any stories in this book are true, some names and identifying information may have been
changed to protect the privacy of individuals.

Cover design: Cindy Kiple
Interior design: Beth McGill
Images: e+/Getty Images

ISBN 978-0-8308-3687-1 (print)
ISBN 978-0-8308-9703-2 (digital)

Printed in the United States of America ∞

**Library of Congress Cataloging-in-Publication Data**
Allen, Daniel, 1959-
  Summoned : stepping up to live and lead with Jesus / Daniel Allen
Jr.
     pages cm
  Includes bibliographical references.
  ISBN 978-0-8308-3687-1 (pbk. : alk. paper)
  1. Men—Religious life. 2. Christian life. I. Title.
  BV4528.2.A45 2015
  248.8'42—dc23
                                                    2014034481

| P | 20 | 19 | 18 | 17 | 16 | 15 | 14 | 13 | 12 | 11 | 10 | 9 | 8 | 7 | 6 | 5 | 4 | 3 | 2 | 1 |
| Y | 32 | 31 | 30 | 29 | 28 | 27 | 26 | 25 | 24 | 23 | 22 | 21 | 20 | 19 | 18 | 17 | 16 | 15 |

To

Lainie

Bobby

Tom

Lana

Terry

Hugh and Matt

Austin

and Trey

who encouraged me

to write.

# CONTENTS

# FOREWORD

I'm forty-seven now. Not too old yet, but not a young man either. Just the right age to know that the most important things in a man's life are what he believes about himself and what he believes about Jesus.

At the age of sixteen I was forced to work a full-time job. My sister was in and out of state mental hospitals and my parents were divorcing. At that time, I had to either bank on my own ability to navigate life alone or I would have to literally and figuratively bank my life on the character of God, which seemed elusive, hard to figure out, and thus pretty tough to orient your life on.

I was out of my league. Try to be godly? Yeah, right. Try not to lust after women? No way. Operate my business with absolute integrity? Who does that? Be different, live supernaturally, be a leader. These were inspiring concepts, but I didn't know where to turn. My heroes were fading, falling out of relationships, failing morally, and soon I forgot that I could be any different.

The only men I found inspiring were MMA dudes that could get kicked in the face and keep their minds straight and their emotions intact. Blokes that had vision and dreams of wild exploits they wanted to pursue and actually did something about it. I wondered, and always have: Where are the real men? Can I be one of them?

It changed for me on a day when one man took me out and summoned me. A summons is a call out of the normal and into something unique, hard, but worth every drop of blood it costs. A summons is a good coach who grabs you by the facemask and while spitting into your helmet, screams something that pushes you beyond yourself. A summons is a woman you care about asking if you're any different than all the other guys. A summons is what every real man needs before you end up like everyone else.

I hope that as you read this book you'll accept the summons. Most won't, but maybe you will. Daniel is a friend and a mentor to me, and I can commend him as a guide that has been where you want to go.

Read on if you want to live the life God dreams for you.

*Hugh Halter*
*Author,* The Tangible Kingdom *and* Flesh
*Founder, Missio*

# INTRODUCTION

*Put aside the Ranger. Become who you were born to be.*

**Lord Elrond to Aragorn, *The Return of the King***

*I run into people my age all the time who just don't have a clue*
*about what God might want for their lives besides*
*grinding it out nine to five at some lame job.*

**Andy, a twentysomething photojournalist**

Everybody has a story. Fans of *The Lord of the Rings* know that Aragorn was born to be a king but was reluctant to step into that role. He knew that the blood of his forefather Isildur, who clutched greedily to power and the desire for immortality, also ran through his veins. Aragorn feared what he might do if tempted by power and titles. It was left to Elrond, lord of the elves, to challenge him to step into his destiny and lead the armies of Middle Earth in battle against the dark lord, Sauron.

Andy has a story too. An award-winning photographer, he was born to tell stories through his talent with light and camera lenses.

He was also born to tell God's story and to help others find the intersection between their story and God's. It pains him to see how some of his friends have not yet made that connection.

I'm wondering about *your story*. Wondering how you understand who you are, why you're here, where your life is headed and who you're becoming. I wonder how you'd answer the following questions:

- If your life keeps going on its current trajectory, where's it headed? How do you feel about where it's headed?

- What do you want to do with your life? What's leading you in that direction? How do you assess whether that's something you're suited to do with your life?

- Whose expectations do you feel you need to satisfy through what you do with your life? Whose voice seems loudest at the moment?

- What do you think about the possibility that Jesus might have a direction for your life? If you believe that Jesus might have a direction, what's been your experience with finding that direction?

- Who are the people in your life who help you sort out such questions? Who helps you make an honest assessment of where you're strong and weak and what you need to work on now?

Here's how others have wrestled with some of these questions: Gene was deciding which college to attend. His high school buddies wanted him to attend the state university where they could all "have fun together partying every weekend and scoring with as many girls as possible." Gene wasn't sure he wanted to do that. Partying was losing its appeal. He liked his friends a lot, but he wanted to follow Jesus too.

John's dad wanted him to learn a trade and was willing to pay all related expenses—as long as he could dictate the trade. If not, John was on his own. His dad had a wonderful plan for John's life and wanted him to follow it. Though John respected his dad, he had no interest in that particular trade, and he resented the pressure he felt from him.

When Keith graduated college, he was expected to go into the family's automobile business. He wanted to do that at first, and he even dreamed of one day running it and owning his own business in a related field. A couple of years later he wanted to work in sales for a multinational corporation. A couple of years after that he wanted to live abroad and "find himself." He recently decided he wants to work with the soil on an organic farm.

Tom was jaded and cynical about the whole "institutional church" scene, but he was a gifted musician and worship leader. He'd been offered a job in a church across the country from where he lived. The job would pay the bills and provide support for his family, but he'd have to uproot them to move there. And he wasn't excited about that church or that city.

Dan had read a book about entrepreneurs and how a lot of startup companies were being sold for boatloads of money. He thought he had a great idea for a startup and went looking for someone to help him write code and develop algorithms. His idea was solid, but his self-discipline was shoddy. He could see the big picture but struggled with taking care of day-to-day details.

Greg had a burning desire to serve in a church and preach every weekend. He thought he was good at connecting with people relationally and at preaching, but in spite of all the résumés he sent out, he wasn't getting any interviews, much less job offers. He felt confused and a little angry with God. He wondered why potential employers couldn't see what he saw in himself. Sure, he was addicted to porn, but he kept that secret.

Pete had an experience with God when he was ten. He felt that God had called him to help people get free spiritually. He wasn't sure what that meant, but he felt a deep drawing to the Holy Spirit and to learn to pray for people. He also loved being outdoors, going on long hikes and doing technical mountain climbs. He was also darn good with a camera; it felt like an extension of himself. He wondered whether what he felt called to do would ever connect with his love for the outdoors and his aptitude for seeing the world through a camera lens.

Can you identify with any of these examples? If so, in what way? Where are you now with these kinds of questions?

I know a lot of men who are hungry to do good, especially men in their twenties and thirties. I've mentored and coached a lot of them during the past couple of decades. Many were working through questions about life, work, leadership and relationships, such as these:

- Life direction: Why am I here? What am I supposed to do with my life?

- Living from an alive heart: What fires me up? Can I trust what I feel?

- Work: Should I take this job or that one? Does it really matter? What if I don't like it?

- In transition: What just happened to my *life*? Why do I feel so *lost*?

- Sin: Why can't I seem to get past these attitudes and appetites that keep tripping me up?

- Friendships: Who will walk through life with me? How honest can we be with one another?

- Leadership: Am I a leader? Do I really want to influence others? Can I get them to follow me? If so, toward what?

Some of those I mentored were juniors in college waking up to the end of life on their parents' payroll—and stressing about what to do next. Some were fresh out of college or a few years out—and either enduring or enjoying their work. Several were married; others were engaged or dating. Some were taking a break from a girlfriend. All of them, not surprisingly, had character flaws and were carrying hurts and baggage from their past. Some were amped up—all gung ho and ready to charge the field. Others were hesitant, wanting to find God's path but feeling unsettled about what might be required of them. Either way, they were hungry for life beyond what they had. They wanted more fraternity with brothers and spiritual fathers. They wanted more of the life Jesus came to bring.

They worked as artists, managers, educators, coaches, sales reps, entrepreneurs, commercial real estate brokers, accountants, architects, pastors, church planters and campus missionaries. They did marathons and triathlons, played soccer and rugby, climbed glaciers, and enjoyed hunting and fly-fishing. They wrote songs and played in bands. They wrote screenplays and made films. Some preferred bourbon and others Scotch. Some preferred hoppy and others malty. A few wanted only sweet iced tea.

I'd like to take some of what I've learned in my relationships with them and share it with you. I'll be talking about life direction, character formation, growing as a leader and connecting with others who can help you on your journey.

To be clear from the outset, here's where I'm coming from: The world is broken; Jesus wants to heal it. Jesus has a role for you in that work, and Jesus is at work even now—in your life story—preparing you for that work.

Not a day goes by without reports on the brokenness of the world—reports of homelessness, poverty, hunger, climate change, contaminated water supplies, the abuse of natural resources, the global HIV/AIDS crisis, the abuse of power, the effects and aftereffects of colonialism, human trafficking, slavery, terrorism, genocide, racism, militarism, displaced peoples, broken families, broken economies, toxic leaders and workplaces, broken educational systems, corporate espionage, moral failures on a grand scale and other blatant manifestations of evil. Some of these tragedies have touched you personally. You might already be working to change them or to mitigate the misery they cause.

Jesus wants to heal the broken world. That's why he came. Jesus came to inaugurate God's kingdom life for all who would receive it, and he called and prepared a dozen followers to join him in that work (see, for example, Matthew 4:18-22; 10:1-14; Mark 1:16-20; John 10:10). He went about preaching, teaching and demonstrating how God's kingdom was actually breaking in through his life and work (Luke 4:14-30). Through Jesus, Paul wrote, God is at work on a grand scale, restoring the cosmos and all that is in it (Colossians 1:15-29). Jesus came to heal the broken world and still works to heal it.

Jesus has a role for you in that work. The apostle Paul wrote that we've been created in Christ to do good works—works prepared in advance for us to do (Ephesians 2:10). Works that renew and restore the world. Works that fix what's been broken. And this work is not just for those with paying jobs in the institutional church or support-based ministries. This work is for all of us and is needed in all sectors of society: the arts, sciences, education, engineering, manufacturing, business, government—you name it. All sectors belong to Jesus, and he summons each of us to work with him in one or more of those sectors.

Jesus is at work even now in your life—in your story—preparing you for that work. He works in your life through significant people, events and circumstances, through your natural abilities and through your spiritual gifts to prepare you for the work he has for you to do. Jesus may have already summoned you to a place in the work he's doing. You might know what it is and you might not, but since he's the good shepherd of John 10, you can trust him to make it clear to you when the time is right.

Perhaps now is the time to get clarity and a path for hearing and following God's call, or to refine and advance what you already know. In part 1 of this book, I share my understanding of the phrase "God's call" and how Jesus might reveal his call to you. I also discuss some of the obstacles that get in the way of accepting a call. Once you hear that summons, the ball's in your court. Will you accept it? Will you surrender to Jesus and his call? Some struggle to do so; others immediately say yes.

Part 2 focuses on our inner lives—our character—and how Jesus heals and shapes us there, how he helps us become those he can entrust with influence. I share some of my brokenness, struggles and lessons learned, not to write a memoir, but in hopes that if I'm open about my baggage, you can be open about yours.

Part 3 introduces some leadership fundamentals to help you get started on your journey of influence. A lot of outstanding books have been written about the nature and practice of leadership. Books like *The Truth about Leadership* by James Kouzes and Barry Posner, and John Kotter's *Leading Change* and Edgar Schein's *Organizational Culture and Leadership* will take you deep and far in understanding a core set of leadership practices and necessary skills. Read those books, or others like them, and profit from them. But also take note of lessons you probably won't find in so-called secular literature.

I'll discuss some of the factors that are especially important for leadership of a spiritual nature (whether you work in a classroom, boardroom, cubicle, garage or design studio, or on a playing field). For example, I comment on getting your direction from God, on the need for dependence on God and on fighting battles of a spiritual nature.

In part 4 you will find encouragement to connect with others Jesus will bring into your life, others who can help you move forward with and sustain you in the work Jesus gives you to do. In particular you'll learn about the types of mentors you'll need at different times and the men who'll help keep your feet on the ground and the fire stoked in your soul—men who'll be your allies in living and leading with Jesus.

Ready? Let's get started.

# PART ONE

# SUMMONED

## Discovering God's Call and Our Life Direction

*Follow me*

*and I will make you*

*fishers of men.*

**Jesus**

*We are listening, always listening for*

*the Divine voice amid the clutter.*

**Richard Foster**

**1**

# WAKE-UP CALL

### You've Been Summoned

*Do not be afraid; keep on speaking, do not be silent . . .*
*because I have many people in this city.*

**Jesus speaking to Paul, Acts 18:9-10**

What does it mean to be called by God? How does calling happen? Is God's call just for religious types or just those into "church work"? What's so special about being called by God? And how can you get clarity on God's call for your life? Let's take a look at these questions.

During the spring semester of my junior year of high school, God came calling. He shattered my sleep early one morning; I woke up at two.

My train of thought went something like this: *Huh. I'm wide-awake. This is weird. I never wake up at two. I sleep through the night then drag myself out of bed to get breakfast before heading off to school. This is not normal.* I looked around the room, wondering what I could do to get back to sleep. Option A: music. Would my tunes help me get back to sleep? Hardly. Option B: My Bible, there on the nightstand by my bed, King James Version, red-letter edition. *That might work. I'll read the Bible for a while; that'll put me back to sleep.*

I thumbed its pages. It fell open to the book of Acts. Two verses stood out, red letters against the white page: "Then spake the Lord to Paul in the night by a vision, 'Be not afraid, but speak, and hold not thy peace: For I am with thee, and no man shall set on thee to hurt thee, for I have much people in this city'" (Acts 18:9-10 KJV). The Lord was speaking to Paul *in the night,* instructing him not to be afraid and to speak. It must have been encouraging to him, but . . .

*This is about more than encouragement for Paul,* I thought. *This has something to do with me too.*

My palms were sweating, my pulse quickening. "Oh crap," I groaned. This was not what I wanted to hear. Ever. Not in the way that I sensed its meaning for me: God *encouraging* Paul, God *calling* me. It was a summons. God was calling me to a specific type of work. In the faith tradition of my childhood and high school years, I understood this to mean that I was being called to be a pastor.

I hadn't asked for the summons; I hadn't gone looking for it. My dad was a pastor, my mom a lay minister, and I was a pastor's kid (along with Jody, my sister, who was two years older). I grew up in a pastor's home where life revolved around the church. A lot of that life was good, but it wasn't the life I wanted in adulthood. I wanted a different kind of future. I wanted to be a lawyer, to drive fast cars, to make a lot of money. That was my version of the American dream.

I often heard people say during my childhood, "I bet he's gonna grow up and be a preacher like his dad." No thank you. No way.

Don't get me wrong. I loved Jesus. I'd had a genuine conversion experience in childhood and was later baptized in water. I generally enjoyed reading the Bible. But called to preach? "Please, Lord, no."

I closed the Bible and put it back on my nightstand. Somehow I managed to go back to sleep. But the gauntlet had been thrown down. The seed planted. The summons issued. And that early-morning wake-up call stayed with me. Haunted me. Little did I know then, but later in life it would be the North Star that would guide me through some serious storms.

## Definitions

To *summon* is to urgently or authoritatively call someone.[1] For example, you could be summoned to appear in court. Or summoned by church bells to prepare for worship. You may have heard a physician being summoned over a public address system in a hospital. I'm using the word in the sense of being authoritatively called by someone. For our purposes here, it means being *summoned* by Jesus—or, if you prefer, *called*.

The words *call* and *calling* come to us from the Latin word *vocatio*, from which we get our English word *vocation*.[2] A vocation is a calling, a recognition that someone (God) or something (a cause, a particular group of people, an opportunity to seize or problem to solve) has taken hold of us and won't let go. It's a summons, if you will. The prophet Jeremiah was called to prophesy to Judah and her surrounding nations, and he described his call as a "fire shut up in my bones" (Jeremiah 20:9).

A calling seizes you, takes hold of you. You don't invent it. It's not the same as thinking logically through a career path. You don't make it up; it comes to you. You might come to understand it as something that's been present in your life for a long time, but even then it's something from outside yourself. As I'm describing it here, it comes from God.

God comes calling.

While the words *vocation* and *occupation* are often used interchangeably, they shouldn't be. They don't mean the same thing. *Occupation* is work we do for a living (a job). Our occupation may or may not allow the expression of our vocation (our calling). *Vocation* is more pointed and specific. A vocation can be fulfilled through a number of occupational expressions (jobs). For example, my calling might be to develop leaders, but I can do that through executive coaching or as a grad school professor or as an abbot in a new monastic community.

Calling is not just for those who believe they're summoned to church work. My friend James feels called to address the global HIV/AIDS crisis. That's his vocation. He's been summoned to help those affected by the crisis and, in particular, to change the way fourth-through sixth-graders perceive the problem. But he's working right now in a grocery co-op—that's his occupation—while he volunteers at a community center to live his vocation. Nehemiah was called to lead a massive public works project. Esther was called to help avert widespread genocide.

## Three Aspects of Calling

Vocation (or calling) has three parts: the summons to *relationship* with God, to *partnership* with God and to *leadership* with God.[3] To say it another way, we're called to live and lead with Jesus for the life of the world. Let's look at each part.

*Called to relationship.* Jesus embodied this desire for relationship in his incarnation and ministry. He emphasized that life with and in God—*relationship* with God—was why he was sent: "For God so loved the world that he gave his one and only Son, that whoever believes in him shall not perish but have eternal life" (John 3:16). "Now this is eternal life: that they know you, the only true God, and Jesus Christ, whom you have sent" (John 17:3). The English word *know* in the previous verse is from a Greek word that refers to intimate experiential knowledge. It's the kind of knowing that a husband and wife have of each other. Here Jesus says that eternal life means this kind of knowing, which happens as we live our call to relationship with God. The apostle Paul put it like this: It is God who has "called you into fellowship with his Son, Jesus Christ our Lord" (1 Corinthians 1:9). The invitation to wonderful fellowship, to knowing God, is the call to relationship.

The call to relationship means to know Jesus, love Jesus, speak with Jesus, enjoy wonderful friendship with Jesus. Some authors refer to it as the *general* call to know and follow Jesus. From Genesis—with Adam and Eve walking with God in the garden—to Revelation and the wedding feast to come, the Bible shows that God seeks *relationship* with people. This call to relationship is woven throughout the Bible's great story.

I accepted the call to relationship with Jesus at a young age, in a worship service. My dad had scheduled a guest speaker for a week of spiritual enrichment meetings (called a revival in the faith tradition of my childhood). At the closing worship service of those meetings, the speaker shared part of the gospel with us. He told us about God's desire for relationship with us—but that our sins had separated us from God. He explained that by confessing our sins to God and turning to Jesus, we could be forgiven. He said that Jesus had died to deal with humanity's sin problem and that by trusting Jesus we could be "born again" into a new life. He invited those who were hearing God's call to come forward, turn to Jesus and receive prayer. I did. I answered that day what I later came to understand as my call to relationship with God through Jesus.

***Called to partnership with Jesus.*** God calls us to partnership in the advancement of God's purposes. It's central to the story that we inhabit. God works in the world through people. Or, as I put it in the introduction, the world is broken, Jesus came to heal it, and he calls us to join him in his work.

This partnership includes the general ways Jesus might lead each of us to serve others, which could include praying for the sick, feeding the hungry, listening to a friend share his pain or joy, loving and nurturing your wife and children or working for the *shalom* of your city. These examples of partnership are common to all of us who follow Jesus. They are part and parcel of our discipleship.

But partnership with Jesus also includes your *specific* mission, your life purpose. It's what God wants you to do with your life, the contribution God has designed you to make. One of my mentors calls it the Ephesians 2:10 life: discovering and doing the good works God has prepared in advance for each of us to do.

We see a summons to a specific call in several places in Scripture. God called Moses to lead Israel out of Egypt, Joshua to lead Israel into Canaan, Samuel to prophesy, Esther to foil Haman's planned genocide, Nehemiah to rebuild Jerusalem's walls and catalyze a spiritual renewal movement, Mary to mother the Son of God, Saul to become an apostle to the Gentiles, and Timothy and Titus to serve with Paul.

Here's how some of the men I've worked with understand their second-order call: Gregg explores larger social issues through filmmaking. Mark helps organizations authentically communicate and connect with their various audiences. Hugh inspires and trains church leaders to create incarnational communities. Matt inspires high school students with a love for science, travel and competition. David works with raw materials—men and concrete—to create artistic hardscapes and give men a chance to go home from work with smiles on their faces. Ben writes songs about the beauty and mystery in life and love. Paul uses photography to help people see the light. Terry strengthens risk-taking kingdom leaders by helping them discover how God is shaping them for an ultimate contribution.

I first understood my specific summons as the call to pastor and preach. The initial summons was what started me on the path to serving full time in church-related ministry. Several years later, the call became even more focused: I was called to equip the church through leadership development, especially with emerging leaders.

As I mentioned earlier, sometimes we get to live out our specific call through our occupation. Sometimes we don't. When we do, it's as if the stars line up and dance for joy. It's like hitting a baseball in the sweet spot. When we don't, it can drain us unless we find a way to make peace with it.[4] When my occupation was in automobile detailing, I wasn't living my vocation through my job. When my occupation was physical education instructor and after-school athletics coach for elementary and junior high students, I wasn't living my vocation through my job. I needed to do those jobs to provide for my family. That work was noble and good, and I made peace with it and did it, even though it wasn't in line with my vocation.

*Called to leadership—to* **leading** *with Jesus.* As we live into our call to relationship and partnership with God, we discover that we're also called to lead—to be a positive influence on those around us. That doesn't necessarily mean we influence entire organizations or cities or regions or countries. We're not all called to leadership in those spheres of influence. But we are called to influence with Jesus, whether it's with a few colleagues at work, our closest friends, our roommates, our family, the board we sit on or the students we mentor.

By *lead* I mean *influence.* In his book *Lead Like Jesus,* Ken Blanchard states that if we seek to influence the thinking, behavior or development of another person or group, we're aspiring to *lead.*[5] At its core, to lead is to *influence.*

And I don't mean occasional instances of influence, like when you suggest beer and burgers, and everybody agrees with you. I'm talking about *ongoing* influence toward a better way, a better future or a more life-giving culture for the group, department or organization—and especially for your family.

We can hear the call to leadership in Mark 1:16-20.

> As Jesus walked beside the Sea of Galilee, he saw Simon and his brother Andrew casting a net into the lake, for they were fishermen. "Come, follow me," Jesus said, "and I will send you out to fish for people." At once they left their nets and followed him.

When he had gone a little farther, he saw James son of Ze-
bedee and his brother John in a boat, preparing their nets.
Without delay he called them, and they left their father Ze-
bedee in the boat with the hired men and followed him.

What's going on here? As herald of the inbreaking of the kingdom,
as initiator of a worldwide restoration movement, Jesus is calling
Simon, Andrew, James and John to relationship ("follow me") and
partnership ("fish for people"), so they will learn from him how to
influence others (leadership). The call is to relationship and partnership, but also to leadership—to influencing others into the life
that Jesus seeks for those who will open their hearts to him.

Does that mean you'll be a gifted evangelist or apostle, like Peter,
Andrew, James or John? Maybe. Maybe not. But you're called to
influence others. To love and serve and listen to them. To be a life-
giving presence for them.

To say it another way, because you're called to lead *with Jesus*,
you're called to lead *for the life of the world.* To influence the well-
being of the people, groups or organizations that you serve. To
work for harmony, justice and right relationships. To set up systems
and structures that are life-giving. To create cultures and environments that dignify others and unleash their creative genius.

This means influencing people toward what the Old Testament
refers to as *shalom*—wholeness, harmony, justice, goodness. The
Jesuits refer to it as the common good. It means leading from a
serving posture and influencing for the well-being of others, for
their sake. It's what Robert Greenleaf referred to in the early sev-
enties as servant leadership. He was taking his cue from Jesus.[6]

We live and lead with Jesus for the life of the world because *that's
what God is doing.* God is bringing the world to life, slowly and
surely, as men and women say yes to God's good news and receive
life in the kingdom. This slow-but-sure restoration to life, this con-

tinual extension of the kingdom, is what noted author Dallas Willard refers to as the divine conspiracy. God is making all things new, bringing them to life, wherever men and women welcome God's loving reign.[7] We join God in making all things new as we lead with Jesus for the life of the world.

## The Dynamic Nature of Calling

God summons us throughout our lives. God's call is dynamic and progressive, unfolding over time. When it comes to our calling, we always work with what my friend Terry Walling calls our best understanding to date. While we may receive an initial summons through which God may start us off toward a general objective (such as reaching these people, starting this company, working in this industry, alleviating suffering), the specifics unfold over time through our ongoing relationship with God.

For example, you might first sense a call to use your music gifts to help people in your local church worship God. After a few years, you may realize it includes resourcing other worship leaders in similar settings. Then it may focus even more specifically on helping worship leaders in South America create revelatory art, including music, to engage young adults in Brazil's urban centers.

## Listening for the Summons

Let's say that you want to hear God's call, or to refine it if you have. Here are five ways that God might speak (sometimes they overlap):[8]

1. through awe-inspiring encounters (think burning bushes and bright lights from heaven);
2. through a growing inner conviction;
3. indirectly, through other people;
4. through providential circumstances; and/or

5. through your recognition of God's shaping of your life—seeing
God at work in your story.

*Awe-inspiring encounters* are unmistakable experiences of God's
presence that show us God is with us and has work for us to do. As
with Moses at the burning bush or Saul on the road to Damascus, God
might meet you in an undeniable, unforgettable, awe-inspiring way.
Such a dramatic calling will shape your life from that point forward.

I've worked with many young adults, especially in Christian
circles, who think God calls only through awe-inspiring super-
natural encounters. I don't blame them for thinking that. The super-
natural encounters get all the press. But we don't see awe-inspiring
experiences in the Bible with Timothy and Titus or with Daniel and
Esther. They were each called, but not in a dramatic fashion.

In interviews with undergrads in courses at Liberty University,
Elmer Towns found that only about ten percent said they were
called to a ministry in a sudden (awe-inspiring) fashion. The majority noted that their call came to them gradually. They experienced a *growing inner conviction* about devoting their lives to a
particular cause or group of people.[9]

At other times, God calls us *indirectly, through other people.*
These are occasions when other people take action on our behalf to
dedicate us to God or recruit us into a specific work, like Hannah
dedicating Samuel, Mordecai engaging Esther's help, Paul re-
cruiting Timothy, or John the Baptist's parents giving him to the
Lord at birth. The calling then becomes actualized when it's accepted and embraced personally.

You could also experience God's call through *providential circumstances.* You might look back at different circumstances in your
life or look around at current factors and conclude that God is directing you toward a particular cause or group of people. This was
the case with Nehemiah when he discovered how poorly Jerusalem
and Judah were faring in the fifth century B.C.

Nehemiah was serving King Artaxerxes, and he had access to the king and the resources of the Persian kingdom. So he found himself providentially in a position to help. His concern for the residents of the city, coupled with his periods of prayer and access to resources, led him to discern God's call to rebuild Jerusalem's walls and to catalyze a spiritual renewal (Nehemiah 1–7).

Finally, God's call emerges when we recognize *God's shaping of our lives*. One of my mentors was guiding me through a life-planning process when he said, "Let's connect the dots, Daniel, of your story. Let's see how God has been at work in your past and how that points to your future."[10] He understood how God uses people, circumstances and experiences to point us toward the work God calls us to do.

Indeed, Dan Allender writes that we discover our calling specifically by listening to our stories: "We begin with our stories, always. So read and reread your story. In due season, some of the patterns and the trajectory of your life will begin to appear through the fog. At first there will be only a shape, but with time, prayer, and reflection, you will see the contours of your path come into focus. . . . We don't find our calling; it finds us."[11]

By reading your story, you can find indicators of what you're passionate about, what your gifts are, how you prefer to interact with others and which experiences have most clearly directed you thus far. Put these together, and you can often start to discern God's call. Chuck Colson realized how God had used his story to prepare him to establish Prison Fellowship.[12] Gary Haugen connected his story, especially his 1994 investigation into the Rwandan genocide, with his call to found International Justice Mission.[13]

Joseph also recognized God's call by looking at how God had shaped his life (see Genesis 37–50). God did this shaping to bring him to a place of leadership in Egypt. God blessed Joseph with dreams, with the capacity to interpret dreams, with access to the

Egyptian Pharaoh, with favor with leaders and with world-class administrative skill.

When Joseph looked back over the events of his life—the painful and the positive—he concluded that God had worked through them to summon him to provide for the Egyptians' and the Israelites' welfare. As he put it to his brothers, who had years earlier tried to take his life and then sold him into slavery: "And now, do not be distressed and do not be angry with yourselves for selling me here, because it was to save lives that God sent me ahead of you. . . . So then, it was not you who sent me here, but God" (Genesis 45:5, 8).

"Not you . . . but God," Joseph told them. His life is a witness to how God uses the events of our lives to direct and guide us. As Dunham and Serven put it, "The truth is, God tends to take us from point A to point Z *through* points B, C, D, E, and so on. In other words, we don't just arrive somewhere; we go through a process along the way."[14] Sometimes God's call becomes clear to us as we reflect on that process, as we see the lessons and turning points of our story.[15]

You've been summoned. Called to relationship, partnership and leadership. Called to live and lead with Jesus for the life of the world. As you say yes to Jesus, the purposes of God will move forward, and the kingdom will extend through your life.

- How has God's call come to you?
- Which parts have become clear to you?
- How are you responding?

# SURRENDER

### Lay Down the Stuff
### That Gets in the Way

*[Jesus] said to another man, "Follow me."*
*But he replied, "Lord, first let me go and bury my father."*

**Luke 9:59**

*But Moses said, "No, LORD, don't send me.*
*I have never been a good speaker, and I haven't*
*become one since you began to speak to me.*
*I am a poor speaker, slow and hesitant."*

**Exodus 4:10 (TEV)**

Miserable, conflicted, bothered and troubled.

That's how I felt the summer after my freshman year of college. I was running from God. I was resisting the two o'clock wake-up call from my junior year of high school. I was rooming with my good

friend Ron and his family in Florida, making decent money for a
college student, working in Fort Lauderdale, hoping for sunshine
and beaches. *But I was working the night shift*—three nights in a row,
by myself from seven to seven, fighting to stay awake in a guard
shack making a railroad bridge go up and down over a section of
the Intracoastal Waterway. I slept during the day when I could've
been at the beach. This went on for much of May, all of June and
July, and part of August—three nights on, three nights off. Ron had
the day shift on the same job.

I had a lot of time to think during those night-shift hours alone.
I knew I was running from God's call, but I couldn't imagine living
the way I thought I'd have to live if I said yes. I was not ready to
accept the summons. Not ready to make a commitment to Jesus
as Lord. I wanted life my way, on my terms. I wanted salvation
God's way, sure. But not life direction God's way. I was not ready
to surrender.

### In Good Company?

The struggle to surrender didn't start with me (obviously). Leaders
in the Bible struggled with their specific callings as well as with
one-time acts of obedience. Moses protested God's call—even
while he knelt barefoot as God spoke to him out of the burning
bush. He didn't want to confront Pharaoh. He told God he wasn't a
good speaker (Exodus 4:10). Jonah ran from God's call. He didn't
want to preach to the Ninevites. He knew that if they repented, God
would forgive them, and he didn't want that. He spent three days in
the depths of misery before he said yes to God, and even then he
continued to be angry with God (Jonah 4:1-2). Jeremiah didn't want
to be God's spokesman. He told God he was too young to speak
(Jeremiah 1:6). The rich young ruler didn't want to sell his possessions and give to the poor (Matthew 19:22).

## The Struggle with Surrender

At one time or another, we all struggle with surrender—with laying down our will. Stuff gets in the way. We're not sure we can trust God. Not sure we want to live God's call. We balk at turning over the steering wheel of our lives, at pledging our commitment to Jesus as King and Lord.

I once heard Terry Walling say that sometimes the only thing worse than being unsure of God's direction is knowing it and then needing to *surrender*, to lay aside whatever keeps us from stepping out to follow God. It's not that God's purposes for us are bad and not for our best; it's that we like to remain in control. Or that we don't trust God's heart.[1]

Surrender means that we give up control, that we deny self and relinquish things like needing to be in charge, needing to have all the answers in advance, needing to look good or to be famous. It means walking with God, often into the unknown. Trusting God to lead and provide. Trusting God to come through.

Of course not everyone struggles to the same extent to accept God's call. Some seem not to struggle at all. You might relish that God has chosen and called you not only to relationship but also to a specific cause or people group. Joshua didn't seem to struggle as Moses did. Elisha asked to inherit Elijah's role and anointing (2 Kings 2:9). Isaiah responded to God's call with "Here am I. Send me!" (Isaiah 6:8). Ezra appears to have readily accepted his call to live and teach God's statutes to Israel (Ezra 7:10). Paul jumped into preaching just days after his surrender (Acts 9:20).

## A Leadership (Lordship) Commitment

Part of my struggle in surrendering was that I had no role models to emulate. I didn't want to become like the ministers I knew. I didn't see anyone I could relate to or aspire to model my life after. Another part of my resistance was that, to accept the summons, I'd have to make a *leadership commitment*—that is, a commitment to Christ as *Lord,* as the *supreme leader* of my life.

We make a leadership commitment when we acknowledge to God our willingness to serve however God leads. As Robert Clinton wrote,

> The heart of the leadership committal . . . is an inward private agreement (though there may be some public stimulus to this) between the potential leader and God. The agreement pledges willingness by the potential leader to be used by God in service for him as the major priority of life. In essence, it is a Lordship decision with regard to service for Christ.[2]

Did you get that? An *agreement* to be used by God, in service to God, as *"the major priority of life."* That's the decision I needed to make. Would God be first—and Daniel second? Would I surrender my will and commit to God's will? Would I do it even if I didn't know how it would unfold?

## The Initial Surrender

Here's how surrender happened for me, when I was finally too miserable to keep running and wrestling. I walked out from the guard shack to the edge of the bridge and knelt down on the gravel between the railroad ties. Then I asked God to do surgery on my heart. I was a weak and fearful nineteen-year-old, but somehow I mustered the courage to say something like this: "Father, I don't want to accept your call. I don't have those desires. But if you'll take my desires and give me yours, then I'll accept your call and serve you." Real man of faith and power, huh?

What happened next was a desire transformation. I kid you not. I knelt down not wanting to accept God's call and stood up having accepted it, because God transformed my desires. It was like God gave me a new heart. This didn't take all my fears and concerns away, but I now had peace for moving forward. I now could trust and follow. I would need to surrender at other times over the next several years, but this was my initial leadership commitment, feeble and shaky as it was.

## Making Your Surrender

We all have stuff that gets in the way of accepting God's call. Stuff that needs to be laid at God's feet and worked through with God. Among other things, I've had to lay down my concern about what others think of me. Early on, it was something like, "He's going to be a *preacher*? He could do much better than that." Then it was, "He's going to that church in Arizona? Isn't that the liberal church that left the denomination?" Then it was, "You're moving your family and infant daughter *where*? And *without* a job? That's pretty foolish. What kind of dad are you?"

Sometimes what gets in the way is what a therapist described to me as "man fears." We all have some form of man fears; some of us are just better at hiding them. Here are a few common ones:

- We don't have what it takes.

- We're not good enough.

- We don't measure up.

- We don't belong.

- We're too far behind everyone else.

- We'll be exposed or found out; others will find out we don't have what it takes.

What could hold you back from stepping out to live God's call? Doubt? Insecurity? Fear of failure? Distrust of God? Holding on to your own dreams? Wanting to look a certain way? Wanting to control the results? Pride?

The act of surrender isn't *complicated*; we don't need ten steps on how to surrender. It can be *difficult,* but Jesus will help you. You

can start by saying, "I want to be willing. Please help my unwill-
ingness. Grant me grace to trust you and give you the stuff that's
getting in my way. Work in me to desire and to do your good purposes." As Tom Paterson points out, surrender happens not just in
our intellect but also in our hearts (our desires). Our hearts must
be willing. Our hearts must make the commitment. Take a look at
Paterson's construct (figure 2.1).[3]

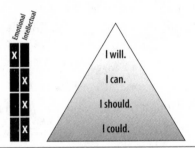

**Fig. 2.1.**

Here's how he puts it: "The bottom three (*could, should, can*) are
all intellectual rationalizations, not commitments. It is important to
think things through. It's why we have minds. But 'I will' is a real commitment. It is emotional."[4] In other words, "I will" is from the heart,
the center of our being (Proverbs 4:23). It's not enough to know that
we could, should or can surrender. We have to put our hearts into it.

We've been summoned to live and lead with Jesus for the life of
the world. Think of the characters in C. S. Lewis's *The Chronicles of
Narnia* or J. R. R. Tolkien's epic *The Lord of the Rings*. Like them, we
have something great and glorious going on all around us. God is
at work, making all things new and inviting us into that work.

- When have you struggled to follow God?
- What stood in your way?
- What could keep you from accepting God's call now?

# PART TWO

# SHAPED

## Cultivating Integrity and Influence

*Follow me*
**and I will make you**
*fishers of men.*

**Jesus**

*Jesus' concern was not with programs to reach*
*the multitudes, but with men whom the*
*multitudes would follow.*

**Robert Coleman**

## 3

# FINDING *IT*

## Focus Where You Are Until God
## Leads You to What's Next

*Whoever is faithful in a very little is faithful also in much;*
*and whoever is dishonest in a very little*
*is dishonest also in much.*

**Jesus in Luke 16:10 (NRSV)**

*It is good for a man to bear the yoke while he is young.*

**Lamentations 3:27**

My friend Tom, a couple of years out of college as I write this, has been searching for *it*—the specific part of his calling: a life purpose. He's in a job that pays well. His company will pay for him to attend business school and then bring him back to a boost in salary and more responsibility in the firm. But that job, that career path, is not *it* for Tom. He feels restless.

Lou feels that way too. He works for a medical orthopedic

company, and he played on a national championship lacrosse team. Women love Lou, and guys have a man-crush on him. He's good at what he does. He's outgoing, smart, winsome. But he feels stuck. He knows what *it* is, but he's not getting to work in that role right now—at least not in a paid position.

We don't always get to do *it* right away. If you're a recent college grad, your first job out of college will probably *not* be *it*, even though you might enjoy the work. It could be *it*, but there's a greater chance that it won't. You might find out later, in retrospect, that it was part of *it*, was pointing to *it* or preparing you for *it*, but that entry-level job was not your specific calling. Your second job might not be *it* either, even though you might be good at it. You'll likely be in your late twenties or early thirties before you discover and are released into the focus of your life's work.

If you're a twentysomething (ages eighteen to twenty-nine) in the United States, you're in a stage that Clark University psychologist and research professor Jeffrey Jensen Arnett has termed "emerging adulthood." This is a period of life characterized by exploration and possibilities, but also by instability and a distinct feeling of being between adolescence and young adulthood.[1] Given these features of life in your twenties, it's natural to work for more than one company as you search for a job that you feel suits who you are and what you care about. In fact, Arnett and his research assistant Joseph Schwab discovered that almost two-thirds of emerging adults have not been able to find "the kind of job they really want."[2] Arnett found that "an unstable economy plus difficulty in finding the 'right' job means that the typical young adult in the United States holds an average of eight different jobs between the ages of eighteen and thirty."[3] Eight different jobs. Does that ring true of your experience? Or the experience of others you know?

## Training Ground

The delay is not just a societal factor; it's also consistent with how God works. Joseph was in his teens when he had dreams about his future, dreams he later came to understand as God-given. He was thirty when he was named prime minister of Egypt. David was in his teens when Samuel anointed him king over Israel. He was close to thirty when he was acknowledged and crowned. What happened in the intervening years for Joseph and David? God trained them, preparing them for the roles they would occupy.

While you're longing to work at *it*, God is at work *in* you. Teaching. Shaping. Building character. Instilling virtues and forming values. Helping you discover who you are and what you're good at, suited for, passionate about. God is teaching you how to work and lead effectively. While it's natural to want to be out there slaying the dragon, God is at work in you, forming a dragon slayer. God is helping you become faithful. To be faithful is to be loyal, dependable, reliable and willing to take risks. You demonstrate faithfulness when you show up, when you keep your word, when you do the work.

Sometimes the formation of faithfulness comes through taking on short-term assignments, like summer internships or study abroad programs. Or short-term leadership roles in music groups, on sports teams or in fraternities. Or trips like Eric took when he walked and photographed his way across Nicaragua, and Joe when he helped lead a short-term project to La Chureca, the garbage dump community in Managua, Nicaragua. At other times, short-term assignments stretch into lengthier roles. Austin served eighteen months with a full-service marketing firm. Patrick worked three years as a barista. David put in five years with a construction firm.

God uses these tasks, assignments, opportunities and experiences—shorter term and longer term—to teach us discipline, commitment and follow-through. In our twenties, we want to go out

and bring down the big moose, bag the trophy elk, change the
world. I admire the passion. But while we're wanting to change the
world, God is at work in us.

Sculpting.

Smoothing.

Stretching.

Strengthening.

Showing us ourselves—the good and not so good.

God shows us what we dread and what we delight in—what we
run to and run from. God helps us grow up. Mature. Become faithful
and trustworthy. Why? So that God can then trust us with larger
projects, delicate situations, broader spheres of influence with
people—with God's *purposes*. God can then trust us to live and lead
well with Jesus for the life of the world. The one who is faithful in
little, Jesus said, can then be trusted with more (Matthew 25:23).

## The Work Matters

We start where we are, doing the work that's been opened to us.
Work is good in and of itself. To work is one of the reasons God
created humankind. Doing good work is one of the ways we reflect
the nature of God, who worked for the six days of creation then
rested on the seventh day (Genesis 1–2). Jesus said that he worked
because his Father was working (see John 5:19-20). When the Jesuit
priest and author Walter Ciszek, a survivor of Russia's Lubyanka
prison and the Siberian Gulag, reflected on the work he could do
*while imprisoned*, he was inspired by Jesus' example:

> There is a tremendous truth contained in the realization that
> when God became man he became a workingman. . . . The
> Gospels show us Christ the teacher, the healer, the wonder-
> worker, but these activities of his public life were the work of
> three short years. For the rest of the time of his life on earth,

God was a village carpenter and the son of a carpenter. He did not fashion benches or tables or beds or roof beams or plow-beams [*sic*] by means of miracles, but by hammer and saw, by ax and adz. He worked long hours to help his father, and then became the support of his widowed mother, by the rough work of a hill country craftsman. Nothing he worked on, as far as we know, ever set any fashions or became a collector's item. He worked in a shop every day, week in and week out, for some twenty years. He did the work all of us have to do in our lifetimes. There was nothing spectacular about it, there was much of the routine about it, perhaps much that was boring. There is little we can say about the jobs we do or have done that could not be said of the work God himself did when he became a man.[4]

So because Jesus worked, we work. By doing so we can become productive, constructive, culture-making contributors to society. We work because work is noble and good.

The Benedictines think so highly of work that they make it part of their four-part way of life (their "Rule"): prayer, study, work and leisure. They work six days out of seven, week after week. Macrina Wiederkehr, a Benedictine nun, speaks of this high view of work when she writes, "Work is a service for the benefit of the entire world. . . . All work is for the purpose of improving life."[5] Through our work, we can make the world a better place. We also provide for our physical and financial needs, for our families and for others in need. In this way we honor God and serve others (1 Thessalonians 4:1-2, 9-12).

### The Way You Work Matters

You still need to eat, right? Pay the bills? You hopefully still want to contribute to the common good, even if you're not yet released into *it*. So in the meantime, recognize that God is using the current circumstances and experiences to shape your life. Then settle in and do the work. Focus on serving faithfully where you are until God leads you to what's next. It's like Dunham and Serven say: "We can't always be *going* somewhere. We need to *be where we are*—one hundred percent—growing in humility, integrity, teachability, and faithfulness."[6]

So, while the work you're doing right now might not be *it* for you, to work as unto God and for the service of others is virtuous. Dig in. Take up the yoke. Embrace the keyboard, the paintbrush, the backhoe, the spreadsheets, the scales, the delivery van, the tool belt or the briefcase—and take up the love of God through all of that.

By developing faithfulness, we build a platform for our lives—a platform of character, courage and competence. Building the platform is consistent with the developmental goals you need to achieve in your twenties. Arnett puts it like this:

> Emerging adulthood is a key time for preparing the foundation for the kind of work people will be doing in their adult lives. This foundation is prepared in part through education, as many emerging adults pursue postsecondary schooling intended to provide them with skills that will be useful in the workplace, and in part through workplace experience, usually through a series of jobs rather than one job over time.[7]

Mark Banschick, a psychiatrist and child advocate, writes in his blog post, "Failure to Launch—Male and Stuck at Home,"

> Your twenties is the beginning of adulthood, an independent life that belongs to no one else but you. It's a time when you construct a future; a platform of sorts that will benefit you later down the road. You get a job, learn new skills and try to make relationships work. . . . In your twenties you build a new adult platform, which is why people are willing to work so hard at this important time in life. You get a skill, a profession,

learn to hold a job and make relationships work. Your new platform provides the structure, funds, food and fun that used to be given to you by your parents.[8]

Meg Jay takes it a step further. Jay is a clinical psychologist who specializes in adult development in general and emerging adulthood in particular. In her book *The Defining Decade,* she both challenges and equips twentysomethings to seize the opportunities offered by the decade of their twenties. One of those opportunities is to take advantage of how your brain is being formed.

> Twentysomething work and school are our best chance to acquire the technical, sophisticated skills needed in so many careers today. . . . As neurons that fire together, wire together, the jobs we have and the company we keep are rewiring our frontal lobes—and these same frontal lobes are, in turn, making our decisions in the office and on Saturday nights. Back and forth it goes, as work and love and the brain knit together in the twenties to make us into the adults we want to be in our thirties and beyond. . . . Twentysomethings who use their brains by engaging with good jobs and real relationships are learning the language of adulthood just when their brains are primed to learn it.[9]

How timely that, during our twenties, our jobs are "rewiring our frontal lobes." When we work on becoming faithful at work, we're enabling the kind of brain-shaping activity that can set us up for a life of greater fruitfulness. So the reasons for settling in to do the work are not just theological and sociocultural but also neurobiological.

In emerging adulthood, then, one of your goals should be to take responsibility for your life—that is, for doing what you can do where you are now. Develop self-discipline and learn to be faithful at work, even if the work is not yet *it.*

Micah settled in and taught high school Spanish while waiting on *it*. Tyler operated a backhoe. Rayburne sold computers. Charles worked for a health food store. John Mark crunched numbers at an accounting firm.

*What happened after that? Eventually* Micah was offered a ministry position with a large church. Tyler was offered work leading a worship arts team at a large church. Rayburne submitted an application for a coaching position and was offered a job coaching football and forming young men. Charles faced his fears and stepped out, with his wife, Corrie, to open a full-service bike/adventure shop. John Mark applied for a position with a commercial real estate firm and lived on ramen soup for a year.

These men settled in and went to work. They took up the yoke of faithfulness formation. And eventually the tide turned for them. It's turned for others too. If you're faithful with little, you can then be trusted with more.

Make up your mind to lean in and give all you can to your work. And get all you can too. Learn everything you can about the functional parts of the job as well as the relational aspects. Watch the leaders. See how they interact with peers and subordinates. Do what you can to contribute to the common good. Add value. Get to the work site before you have to. Be one of the last to leave. Double-check your work. Choose to trust God's work in you. It's for your good and is part of your shaping. If you do your work as unto the Lord and for the Lord's pleasure, that's even better (Colossians 3:23).

When the time is right, God will release you more fully into *it*. Let me rewrite that sentence like this: when *God's time* is right, God will release you more fully into *it*. Only God knows the right time. You'll probably get restless and impatient, but you've surrendered, and now it's time for training. You might get disillusioned and be tempted to give up, to despair, to walk away from God's call. Better people than us have given place to confusion and discouragement and given up. Please don't! Your place needs you, but it needs a tempered you, a faithful you. If you come away from the training ground walking with a limp, that's a good indicator of a more fruitful future.

John Mark hated crunching numbers, but he learned to show up and do the work. Tyler cursed that backhoe, but he learned to pay attention to details. Rayburne wanted to work with young men, not sell computers, but he surrendered. Each of these young men grew. They learned humility, patience, discipline, perseverance, how to relate to peers and supervisors. They learned what they were good at and not good at, what they cared about and what they didn't. God was shaping them. They took up the yoke, and that was a good thing. Remember, God is shaping you. Preparing you. Instead of asking, "When do I get to do *it*?" ask, "Lord, am I becoming the person you're shaping me to be?"[10]

- Where are you with finding *it*?
- With leaning in and doing the work?
- With learning to be faithful and to focus where you are?

# 4

# PORN

## It's Time to Come Clean;
## No More Hiding and Pretending

*But I tell you that anyone who looks at a woman lustfully*
*has already committed adultery with her in his heart.*

**Jesus in Matthew 5:28**

Work is not the only place where God is shaping you; God is also shaping you in your so-called private life. Case in point: Porn. This chapter is not about porn *per se*. It's about character formation—who you are and what you do when no one's looking. But my experience with porn illustrates some of the ways God shapes character. In particular, that character is formed as we listen to God and do what God says.

I started using porn my senior year of high school. Using porn led to masturbation. Some people believe masturbation is okay—normal even—in human sexual development. For me, what I was doing was wrong. I was an eighteen-year-old seeking to follow Jesus, and masturbation always included a fantasized sexual encounter with the woman on the page.[1] That was sexual immorality. I was looking at a woman lustfully. I knew it, and I felt guilty about it. But I was hooked on a feeling, and try as I might, I couldn't—or didn't—stop. Not until nine years later.

My first opportunity to stop came shortly after I bought my first magazine. I came home from school one day. Walked into the house as usual. I was hungry, so I walked into the kitchen for a snack. And there stood Marjorie, my mother, hands on hips, with a stern look on her face. "Daniel, I was down praying today," she exclaimed, "and the Holy Spirit told me to go look in the bottom left drawer of the dresser in your bedroom, and *that* is what I found!" She was pointing at a magazine.

My mom—a praying woman if ever there was one. Her dark eyes could narrow into a single steely gaze that could rival a sermon by Jonathan Edwards.

Whether the Holy Spirit actually spoke to her, I don't know. Maybe she was just doing what concerned moms do and checking up on me. What I do know is that right then I had the opportunity to come clean. Maybe even to be cleansed. Healed. As James says, "Confess your sins to each other and pray for each other so that you may be healed" (James 5:16).

But I didn't come clean; I didn't bring my sin into the light. I went darker. I lied.

That's what we often do when we're afraid of what might come next, right? We squirm. Wriggle. Shuck and jive. Look for a way out. Nuance it. "I bought that magazine because of the article on that car, Mom." (The magazine had an article on the Alfa Romeo GT Spider.) "I haven't looked at the pictures."

Yeah, I had read the article, but I bought the magazine to fuel my fantasies. I looked longingly at every picture. In lying to my mother, I missed the opportunity to come clean—and to be cleansed. In lying to her, I rejected an opportunity to develop integrity. God was seeking to train me, to form character in me. But at the time I didn't realize it was God. I thought it was my mother. I surely didn't want to be trained by my mother. Not in this area.

## Integrity

Years later I learned that the episode with my mother was an integrity check.[2] God uses an integrity check to evaluate and reveal the intent of our heart—the consistency between our inner convictions and outward actions—and to serve as a foundation from which God can expand our capacity for influence.

The word *integrity* is related to the word *integer*. An integer is a whole number, not a fraction or decimal. An integer is undivided, complete in itself. To have integrity is to be the same through and through, front to back, in private and public, inside and outside. God will intervene in our lives to shape our integrity—that is, the consistency between our inner disposition and our outward behavior.

In my heart and through my prayers, I had been saying to God that I loved God and wanted to follow Jesus, that I wanted to be truthful and honest. On the outside, I was using porn and lying to my mother. That's inconsistent. Divided. I said one thing but did another.

For those of us summoned to live and lead with Jesus, character formation is central to our development. As one of my mentors puts it, integrity is the *foundation* of godly character. In the majority of failures in leaders' lives, it's poor character that trips him or her up. Poor character can lead to several types of leadership failures—not just sexual sins, but family problems, greed and other financial abuses, the misuse of power, pride and ceasing to respond positively to God's shaping work.

## Take Two

Back to my sexual sin. Roll the tape forward nine years and to another opportunity to come clean. This time God would test my obedience as well as my integrity. I was in my second year of seminary after four years at a Christian liberal arts college and three years as a full-time pastor to high school students. I'd been married for just over five years. The fantasy-based masturbation had continued during those years. One night, Lainie and I were having two of our closest friends, Lance and Linda, over for dinner and prayer. We'd known them for years. They were honorary aunt and uncle to our daughter.

After dinner, we settled into the living room to pray for one another. I stopped by the bathroom first, and as I was washing my hands I "heard" a thought. It was an instruction, actually. I'm putting it in quotation marks because, though it wasn't audible to my ears, it was audible to my mind: "I want you to go confess your sexual sin to Lainie, Lance and Linda. Ask them to pray for you."

Again, here I'm not debating the question of whether masturbation itself is sin, and in what cases it might or might not be. For me it was. I was fantasizing and committing adultery in my heart.

"Do what? Confess to *Lainie*? And Lance and Linda? Really?"

"Yes."

I swallowed. Or tried to. I had a huge lump in my throat and big-winged butterflies banging the walls of my stomach. My hands were shaky. I stared at myself in the mirror, trying to muster up courage. God was intervening in my life, calling me to obedience and inviting me to purity.

"I have something I need to say," I said. "It's difficult for me to share." They sat there quietly, looking at me. No one spoke. "There's something I struggle with that I need to confess. For several years now I've been in bondage to pornography and masturbation. I don't know how to get free. I don't know how to help myself, but I need to confess my sin and struggle to you. I know that I need prayer, and I hope that you'll pray for me tonight."

I felt awkward and exposed but somehow relieved too, like I'd taken a heavy pack off my back after a long uphill hike. Lainie was shocked and hurt. Lance and Linda were shocked too, and embarrassed for me. "We're sorry for your struggle," they said. "And we will pray for you tonight. Right now."

They didn't ask a lot of probing questions; they didn't shame me. They prayed for me, and that night I was set free from years of bondage to fantasy-based masturbation, to a type of soft-porn sexual immorality. I was given an opportunity to "come clean" (confess and repent openly) and "be cleansed" (set free). That night God intervened, and I somehow said okay. God set me free from a sin that I could neither handle nor heal on my own. In doing that, I got a taste of God's kingdom.

Could that intervention have come at any other time in the intervening nine years? Probably. Could God have chosen to set me free in some other way? Probably. Why wasn't I set free any of the other times that I'd cried out to God and swore I'd never look at porn or masturbate again? Why wasn't I set free any of the other times when I pleaded with God to take away the sin and struggle—and promised that I'd stop? I honestly don't know. But I do know that something inside me shifted that night. On that night, I was set free.

### Shaping Our Will

On that night, I also obeyed God. Obedience is one of the foundational virtues that Jesus forms in those he calls. He gives us the strength to obey as we make the choice to obey. Obedience is one of the chief ways we demonstrate our love for God. Not singing Christian songs. Not going to church services. Not having quiet times. Not taking mission trips or planting community gardens. All of these are good, but hear what Jesus said: "If you love me, keep my command" (John 14:15).

Obedience is important for all who follow Jesus, but it's especially important for those who lead. God will shape your character through obedience checks. They test how you will respond to what you sense God asking you to do or become (for example, more truthful or loving or humble or kind).[3]

The focus of your obedience checks depends on the instructions God gives you. God might teach you about obedience in the areas of possessions and giving, about the choice of a spouse, about the timing of a project, about your willingness to trust a truth God has shown you, about your willingness to forgive or to right a continuing wrong. What God is shaping in us is our capacity to recognize God's voice and then to *obey*. First we learn to obey, then we model it and can call others to obey (to follow God).

For example, God told Abraham to sacrifice Isaac (Genesis 22); Joshua to circumcise Israel's soldiers (Joshua 5); Ananias to find and pray for Saul (Acts 9:1-17); and Peter to eat what he understood to be unclean, setting the stage for his interaction with the Roman centurion, Cornelius (Acts 10). In each instance, these men obeyed.

An obedience check has three parts: an instruction from God, your response and the results. In the examples above, we see a clear instruction from God and a positive response from the person, resulting in the forward movement of God's purposes. Sometimes, however, leaders choose to disobey God's clear instructions, like Moses when he struck the rock instead of speaking to it (Numbers 20:6-13); like Saul when he didn't completely destroy the Amalekites (1 Samuel 15; 28); and like Jonah when he refused to preach to the Ninevites (Jonah 1). In each of these cases, the results were negative. Moses, Saul and Jonah were disciplined for their disobedience.

If we're going to live and lead with Jesus for the life of the world, we must learn to obey (to follow) Jesus. Ideally, we learn to obey out of deep love and respect for our great King, who works to restore all things and who is by nature "Love loving."[4]

We must learn to recognize and obey God's voice to become leaders who God can entrust to influence others to fulfill God's purposes. We must model obedience if we expect others to obey God or to one day want to follow us. To say it another way, God intervenes in our lives and invites us into a love relationship. And in that love relationship, God invites us into what is best for all concerned. And what is best? That we walk with our Father like Jesus did: in obedience.

## Purity Matters

While we're on the subject of character, let's take a look at purity. This gets a bit complicated since we've come to faith in different theological traditions within the church, from Orthodox to Coptic, Catholic to Protestant. We've grown up in different cultures with different views on what constitutes morality and ethics. Some of us have been burned by legalism and abuses inflicted in the name of holiness. Others of us read into Paul's instructions to make them mean whatever we want them to mean in order to justify exercising our "freedom" (for example, see Romans 14; 1 Corinthians 8:1-13).

Theologians and biblical scholars don't always agree on what purity is. And through the influence of postmodernity, we've ditched absolute truths in favor of moral relativism: you do what works for you, and I'll do what works for me. In the kingdom, however, purity *matters*.[5] It especially matters for those of us who lead. Paul said as much to Timothy, his young associate:

> In a large house there are articles not only of gold and silver, but also of wood and clay; some are for special purposes and some for common use. Those who cleanse themselves from the latter will be instruments for special purposes, made holy, useful to the Master and prepared to do any good work.
>
> Flee the evil desires of youth and pursue righteousness, faith, love and peace, along with those who call on the Lord out of a pure heart. (2 Timothy 2:20-22)

We're called to make ourselves clean from all those evil things out of devotion to Jesus. Called to purify ourselves and to put ourselves in a place where we can be used for every good deed. As Ignatius of Loyola put it, we are to detach from the thoughts, attitudes and actions that hinder our love for Jesus and to take up those that deepen it. We do that by *cooperating* with what Jesus reveals to us and by *cultivating* our love relationship with him.

I can't name the places of impurity in your life, but Jesus can. Why not ask him, and see what he shows you? Why not ask him in the company of some of your brothers who are on the journey with you? Together we can see what on our own is often muddy. And we can see what we have been trying to justify and rationalize.

## Help for Addressing Porn

Let's go back to our discussion of porn for a moment. If using porn *is* an issue for you, here are a few strategies that might help you address it: understand your motives, involve skilled helpers and lean into grace.

First, your motive. What do you think fuels your use of porn? What drives fantasy-based masturbation? Could it be a desire to prove yourself? Could it be a longing for intimacy, a longing for heart-to-heart companionship? Is it ultimately your longing for God? Like the prodigal son of Luke 15, are you longing to come home to our Father?

Scriptures say we're hardwired for intimacy. For knowing and being known. For loving and being loved at the deepest levels. God made us that way (Genesis 1–3). It's one of the ways we reflect the image of God.[6]

But instead of seeking intimacy with Jesus, a group of friends or our spouse, we seek it through pornography. This is not an attempt to condemn—not after my nine years of bondage. I'm just thinking it might help us if we can move from symptoms to underlying causes—if we can understand our motive, not just the temptation that the tempter brings into our lives and not just the sin of lust. What drives it; what lies beneath it. What moves us to go there, besides hormones and brain chemistry.

I'll ask again. Could it be that we're lonely? Longing for deep friendships? And why don't we have those? Maybe it's that we *don't know how* to know others and allow them to know us. Maybe we haven't seen it modeled. Or we haven't been taught. Or we've been hurt when we've tried to get to know others.

Maybe we're *afraid* to open up, to let others know us. If we don't like ourselves, how can we expect others to like us? I'm not talking about acquaintances here. I'm not referring to the guys in your fraternity that you play video games with, watch sports with, drink beers with. I'm not talking about the guys in your Bible study that you meet with to discuss ideas and concepts. I mean other men who know you in the places that you're scared to talk about, afraid to admit—the dark and secret places.

Could it be that porn is *less threatening than real intimacy*? Does it make you feel less vulnerable? Is it less demanding? Is it just easier, in the short term, to go there? Could it be that it's a place where we think we can prove our sexual prowess, show our strength or have our longings for adventure satisfied?

If we can determine our motives, perhaps we can get further along in finding freedom. I sure as heck wish I'd had someone who knew me help me with my struggle. But I had no one to talk to—no one I knew about, anyway. The guys I knew weren't talking about such struggles. But if we don't understand motives, we're more likely to be dealing with symptoms rather than with what drives our use of porn.

Skilled helpers are a second source of help. I'm thinking of three men right now who battled sexual sin with the support of skilled helpers. Each of them almost lost his marriage. To their credit, they chose the difficult and costly path of seeking professional help. They met with skilled helpers who had studied the complexities of the human heart and psyche as well as the place of sexuality within the complexities, and they were able to help those men sort it out and find healing.

Eric is one of those men. He got help for his porn addiction when he confessed to the elders of his church and enrolled in a rehabilitation program for sex addicts. His elders stood with him in his struggle, and skilled helpers in the program helped him see the underlying issues that drove his behavior. His wife was devastated when the truth came out, but through prayer, the support of her friends, her love for Eric and the steps he was taking, she hung in with him and learned to accept him in spite of his brokenness and sin. In time their love grew, and their marriage was healed.

A third source of help is God's grace. For nine years I struggled with sexual sin—during college, while youth pastoring and in my first several months of seminary. And all that time, God loved me. God didn't condone my sin, but knew me and loved me. I don't get that—why God didn't throw me out, shut me up or expose me along the way.

I'm learning that it's because God takes the long view with us. God is longsuffering toward us. These are expressions of God's grace. Maybe what you especially need is to throw yourself onto this grace—to ask God to work in your life to set you free. This is not a striving in your own willpower, but an intentional and daily surrender to grace that can sanctify and sustain you.

Porn has incredible power to wreck your life. It's an empty sham and will ravage those you care about most deeply. It won't give your heart what it's ultimately looking for. It's a place to hide and pretend. It will wreck your character, if not your life.

Again, the point of this chapter has not been porn but character formation, including core components of character like integrity, obedience and purity. God shapes our character, using mothers, fathers, spouses and friends in that shaping work. God does it for our sake, for theirs and for the sake of the worlds we inhabit and influence. God calls us and God shapes us, especially our character—that is, who we are and what we do when no one's looking.

- Where do you see God shaping your character?

- How are you responding?

- Where do you see fault lines in your character?

- What could you do to strengthen them?

# RELATIONSHIPS

## Do the Hard Work, Like Forgiveness

*And when you stand praying,*
*if you hold anything against anyone, forgive them.*

**Jesus in Mark 11:25**

*Forgiveness is not about justice; it is about healing.*

**James Bryan Smith**

Lance hit me with a low blow, a verbal haymaker. He stunned me, knocking the breath right out of me. He wasn't being malicious and wasn't trying to hurt me. He didn't relish telling me what he saw, but he said it anyway. He told me that I had a problem with unforgiveness.

That was the third time I'd heard the message that week. Once again, God was shaping me, this time in the area of relationships.

Lance and Linda were over for dinner. It was early on a Friday evening. Lance and I were outside grilling burgers and got around to discussing some of the latest pain in my life. Lainie and I had begun to see a marriage counselor and were hitting on some core issues. She had pointed out to our therapist that I acted like I didn't need her, like I could do life perfectly fine without her.

That was an understatement. And it was truthful. I was guarding my heart because she had hurt me eight years earlier, a few months into our dating relationship. I had nursed the hurt, which had grown into a sizable tree of bitterness, resentment and unforgiveness. Thankfully, Jesus came looking for me—with a chainsaw and a stump grinder. At least that's how it felt. It took three nudges to get my attention.

Jesus wanted to talk about relationships, in particular my relationship with Lainie—and my unforgiveness. *What?*

## Three Nudges

Earlier that week, I had been doing some devotional exercises for a seminary class I was taking. The Scripture assigned for my reading was Matthew 5:21-24:

> "You have heard that it was said to the people long ago, 'You shall not murder, and anyone who murders will be subject to judgment.' But I tell you that anyone who is angry with his brother or sister will be subject to judgment. Again, anyone who says to a brother or sister, 'Raca,' is answerable to the court. And anyone who says, 'You fool!' will be in danger of the fire of hell.
>
> "Therefore, if you are offering your gift at the altar and there remember that your brother or sister has something against you, leave your gift there in front of the altar. First go and be reconciled to them; then come and offer your gift."

I had taught from these verses as a youth pastor. I knew they spoke of right relationships. But right then they were speaking to *me*. In my case, it wasn't that someone had something against me, but that I was holding something against someone else. Nudge number 1. Jesus was talking to me about my heart and the hurt I was holding against Lainie. Jesus was saying I needed to forgive her. A couple of days later, I was watching television, flipping channels. I came across the local Christian station, which normally didn't capture my attention. I recognized the host of the program. He'd been a guest preacher one weekend at the church I had worked at in Phoenix. I decided to check out what he had to say.

Turns out he didn't have much to say at all, as the host. But his guests were John and Paula Sandford, who'd done extensive work on—and were speaking that day about—unforgiveness and the damage it causes. Nudge number 2. And Lance was nudge number 3.

Jesus had me. It was time to deal with the unforgiveness thing. I knew that I needed to obey, but I didn't want to. When I held on to the hurt and unforgiveness, I had power. I could use that power to protect myself. I could use it to punish Lainie—in a Christianly passive-aggressive manner, of course. That was the primary way I'd learned to deal with conflict.

But Jesus loved me too much, loved her too much and loved our daughter too much not to address my issue. So he called me out and invited me into healing. It was another obedience check, another test of my character.

Jesus worked with me, and I skittishly worked with him. Forgiveness opened the door and paved the way for love to grow and my character to deepen. Here's some of what I discovered about forgiveness in this situation: First, it's a choice, an act of the will. I didn't feel like forgiving Lainie. I had been in a vulnerable place early in our relationship, and she had wounded me deeply. I had given her my heart, and she had walked on it. If forgiveness was going to happen, I'd have to *choose* to forgive her.[1]

You may be wondering why it took so long for me to deal with the issue. I'm not exactly sure. Probably because I was clueless about the hurt. I had to be one of the least self-aware twenty-seven-year-olds around. I didn't have a spiritual director, didn't take time for self-reflection and had not learned to journal. And it would be a few more months before my therapist enabled me to expand my "feelings repertoire" beyond the rudimentary mad, sad and glad. I had just stuffed it all. And I'm pretty sure I had refused Jesus' earlier invitations to deal with it. I thought Lainie was the problem, not me. *Fix her, and we'll be okay. I didn't do the hurt; she did.* I was justified, right?

Hurt, yes. Justified, no. Not in what I was doing. Not in the way I was treating her, holding it against her. Yes, I loved her. But, boy, did we have a dysfunctional dance going on: "I love you; come closer. No, not really; back off." All unspoken, of course.

Here's another thing I learned about forgiveness: Jesus can help me. He knew I was afraid. He knew I didn't know what was on the other side of the forgiveness bridge. For all I knew, it could have been the proverbial bridge to nowhere. It could have led to even more pain. Jesus gave me strength to make the choice. He helped me acknowledge, feel and grieve the wound. I felt betrayed at the time. I felt vulnerable. But little by little I was opening my heart to Jesus, and he was helping me choose to forgive.

I also learned that forgiveness is reserved for hurts caused by injustices, betrayals, abuse. The guy who cut me off in traffic? He didn't need to be forgiven, but excused.[2] I could excuse his rude behavior. And when Lainie put my wool slacks in the dryer, and they shrunk by a third, that was an honest mistake on her part. She didn't need to be forgiven, but excused.

And I learned that forgiveness doesn't always lead to reconciliation. It takes two to reconcile. Two to put things right between them. Two to be present and willing to reconcile. Jesus was leading me to confess my hurt and repent of my wrongdoing—and to ask to be forgiven. Then to seek reconciliation.

Thankfully, Lainie went there with me. She listened to me as I explained my hurt from that years-earlier episode. She didn't remember it, but she listened to me and believed me. She apologized to me. I apologized to her. I confessed my sin of unforgiveness to her. I told her that she was right, that I had been treating her like I didn't need her. The hurt was the reason. The hurt and my sin.

She forgave me. And when she did, I felt it in my bones. I experienced God that day and God's grace to me through her. Lainie and I reconciled. Jesus healed my heart. Jesus set me free—again. He invited me into obedience and walked through it with me. He was once again summoning and shaping me to step up to live and lead with him—this time through forgiveness.

## Help for Relationships

Jesus restores, heals and helps us in our weaknesses and with our sin. He teaches us about relationships and helps us make them right. He especially does this with those he's calling to lead, those he's calling to influence others, because relationships are central to leadership.

When we're at odds with Jesus, our relationship with him suffers. When we're at odds with others, those relationships suffer. When relationships suffer, the capacity for influence is diminished. How are your relationships going? Where do they need help?

Here are some other insights you might find helpful in your relationships. Try them on and see if they help you.

*Use AHEN.* The next time you feel angry, remember these four letters: AHEN. I learned these from David Gatewood, one of my mentors at Arcadia Christian Fellowship (ACF) when I worked there as teaching pastor. David was a marriage and family therapist, a trainer of other therapists and an owner of a counseling practice. He was also an elder at ACF, and he taught me to notice that when anger (A) is in play, I need to look beneath it. Sometimes lurking beneath anger is a hurt (H), and hurt often comes from an expectation (E) that was not met or a need (N) that was not fulfilled.

Each of these was true in what happened between me and Lainie in that early episode. I was angry and sought to protect myself and punish her. I was hurt because I had expected to be treated in a certain way. I had needed her to be there for me in a certain way. The expectation was not met. And the need was not fulfilled. You might question whether my need was valid. Maybe it was; maybe it wasn't. But it was real to me, and she understood it when we discussed it eight years later.

*Talk about it.* Communicate. Effective communication is a *skill* you can learn. Some people are born talkers, but that doesn't mean they're effective communicators. Others are better at listening, but that doesn't mean they can clearly get across what they think and feel about a given issue.

I know communication is a skill, because my marriage counselor had us practice. And practice. And practice. We started with exercises that lasted ten minutes each. For ten minutes, Lainie would talk and I would listen. No interruptions. And I could ask only specific questions at the end of the ten minutes. Then it was my turn to speak, and she would listen. We worked our way up to ninety minutes each. I thank God for the grace that kept us together and for a therapist who patiently and skillfully helped us learn to love each other better through better communication.

Effective communication happens when we reach mutual understanding—when we each *understand* what the other person is trying to say. What the other person feels and thinks. And what the other person wants to do about it, if anything. In other words, we hear the total message she is trying to get across.

What makes effective communication possible? Time, place, desire, energy and a good framework. Healthy communication takes *time*, especially if we're discussing a sensitive issue. We need a *place* conducive to speaking and listening, and we have to *want* to engage well with the other person. But even if we have the time, place and desire, if we lack *energy* for it, it won't happen. Lainie and I have learned that our energy for effective communication begins to wane around ten at night, so we've agreed not to discuss sensitive or important issues after that time.

Stephen Covey set forth a communication framework built on two fundamental practices: seeking first to understand what the other person is trying to share, then seeking to be understood as you share your thoughts and feelings. You seek to understand through active listening. You seek to be understood by being aware of where you're coming from and then using "I" messages to share your perspective.[3]

**Assume miscommunication.** Somewhere along the way your interpersonal train is going to run off the rails. You and your boss are going to get crossways in a conversation. Or you and your girlfriend. Or you and your wife. Or you and your children.

When that happens, instead of assuming what a jerk he or she is, assume miscommunication. Instead of getting defensive, instead of blaming, start by assuming you didn't understand each other. You'll think you heard and understood; she will think she heard and understood. But you totally misunderstood each other. Even with all our practice, I still hear Lainie say way too much, "Yes, honey, those were my words, but that's not what I *meant*." We both get lazy and slack off on seeking to understand and then to be understood.

**Give others the benefit of the doubt.** This insight is related to assuming miscommunication, but it's more specific to intent (what you think they're trying to do) and identity (your assessment of their character). For example, if your boss is grumpy, you can assume (a) he's just a jerk; (b) she's out to get you; (c) he's actually feeling discouraged and isn't sure how to talk about it; or (d) she just came out of a difficult conversation with a colleague.

Option A takes a negative view of who he is as a person. Option B imposes a negative motivation on her. Options C and D give the benefit of the doubt. They maintain belief in his or her dignity as a person. They keep the door open for communication and help build trust.

To sum up, I've learned that we can strengthen our relationships by using the AHEN tool, by talking about what's troubling us, by assuming miscommunication and by giving each other the benefit of the doubt. If we use these tools, we can decrease friction in our relationships and perhaps even decrease how often we hurt each other.

We can also strengthen our relationships by having friendships in which we can speak truth to each other. Turns out that Lance's low blow was not a low blow at all. It was a helpful dose of truth. I had a problem, but little did I know that owning that problem and stepping into it with Jesus would bring me into healing and transformation. I'm deeply grateful for the word Lance brought to bear in my life that day and for the way Jesus loved me through him.

- How are relationships going in your life?
- What could you do to strengthen them?
- What might Jesus be saying to you about forgiveness?

# 6

# BAGGAGE

### Get the Help You Need to
### Deal with Your Stuff

*When Jesus saw him lying there and learned that he had been
in this condition for a long time, he asked him,
"Do you want to get well?"*

**John 5:6**

*You become what you choose to carry from your past.*

**James Ryan Dorsey**

We all pick up baggage in life: hurts we've suffered, lies we've believed, unhealthy ways of relating we've learned, unresolved mis-
understandings with those closest to us. We've picked up baggage
from our families, our friends, our culture, bullies and the sinister
forces of darkness. We carry it with us until we unpack it and work
through it. If we don't work through it, the baggage ends up
holding us back and hurting those around us.

Susan, our marriage counselor, turned up the heat on me one day. "We've spent a lot of time, Daniel, looking at Lainie's issues, working on her stuff. Now I'm wondering about your stuff. I'm wondering what you bring to the marriage that keeps you guys stuck. What do you see?"

What did she mean, *my* stuff? I didn't have any stuff—well, other than the unforgiveness, but I had worked through that. I loved Jesus, Lainie and our daughter. *Just fix my wife, and the marriage will be fine. After all, I forgave her. What else could there be?* As it turns out, quite a bit. God was still shaping me.

## Some of My Stuff

Here's some of the baggage I discovered I'd brought into our marriage: shame, the three rules and a wounding.

**Shame.** While guilt is the feeling that we've *done* something wrong, shame is the belief that we *ourselves* are wrong. Shame is a toxic rot in the pit of your stomach. It's hands inside your skull, squeezing your brain. It's tapes that play constantly in your mind, pointing out your every flaw and shortcoming.

While guilt says, "I did something wrong," shame says, "I myself am wrong."[1] I've not yet ferreted out everything that sent me that message, but some of it came from comparing myself to others. My family life to theirs. My lot in life to theirs. Some of it was demonic. Some of it was probably neurological, based on how my brain was developing.[2]

Peers at school made matters worse. Middle school kids are world class at finding and exaggerating flaws. So while I did grow up with parents who loved and cared for me, I also grew up in a pastor's home (strike one, in the eyes of my sixth- through eighth-grade classmates); a *Pentecostal* pastor's home (strike two); and in what felt to me like a *poor* Pentecostal pastor's home (strike three).

- "Your dad's a pastor? So, what does he really do?"

- "What's your dad's church? Never heard of it."

- "Oh yeah. My dad says you guys are the tongue talkers and holy rollers."

- "Hey, Daniel, didn't you wear those same pants yesterday?"

- "Why doesn't your mom wear makeup? Why does she wear her hair like that?"

- "Why does your sister always wear dresses?"

- "What do you mean you can't go to movies and dances? Wait, you can't go to parties either?"

That was my world. Shame based. I brought shame-based me into my marriage, and the shame kept me in hiding. It kept me fearful of rejection and conflict. So instead of facing an issue head on, I'd let it simmer and I'd get passive-aggressive. On occasion, I'd blow up and slam doors. Whenever I sensed Lainie making some type of putdown or questioning one of my decisions, it would inflame the shame place, feed it and fuel my fear.

**The three rules.** Mixed in with the shame were three rules I learned growing up: Don't feel. Don't talk about it. Don't rock the boat. I'm not sure which rule came first. They were intertwined. They were related to growing up in a parsonage, thinking the eyes of church people were constantly scrutinizing me. I internalized the need to be perfect, to be the model pastor's son.

The rules sounded like this:

- "Don't feel angry. God won't like that."

- "Don't talk about the tension you feel at the dinner table. No, wait. Don't even feel the tension. Deny it. If you feel it and talk about it, that'll rock the boat, upset the surface calm."

- "Don't talk about church people. Don't talk about church issues. That would be disrespectful."

I brought the three rules into my marriage and heard messages in my head like these: Don't feel hurt about what Lainie just said. Don't feel needy. Don't talk about your needs with her. Don't rock the boat. You know how she is; she'll fly off the handle and get all angry or pouty. Can't have that. Keep the peace.

Marriage counseling helped me rewrite a lot of these rules. Our therapist helped Lainie and me learn new ways to relate, communicate, resolve conflict and fight fairly. I'm pretty sure that if God had not brought Susan into our lives, or someone like her, we'd have ended our marriage about six years into it. The three rules guaranteed conflict and crisis. So did the wounding.

**Wounding.** I was wounded by something I experienced after a kidney surgery in the third grade. Here's the short version of the story: I'd had several bladder infections, and since boys aren't supposed to have a lot of bladder infections, my pediatrician referred me to a urologist for specialized treatment. The urologist was also puzzled, so after running some tests that were inconclusive, he recommended exploratory surgery. He needed to see for himself what was causing my problems.

In layperson's terms, what the urologist found was not a functioning kidney but a "water sack." It was a breeding ground for infection and the source of my excruciating side pain and repeated infections. So he removed it. But when he did, he took away my capacity to play contact sports and to serve in the military. That really, really bothered me in high school and beyond. But that's a different part of my story.

I came through the surgery just fine and endured other procedures that went along with it (enemas, catheters, stitches and nausea from anesthesia, to name a few). And I missed about three weeks of school. Here's the wounding part: On one of my first days back in class, our teacher was taking us through our various subjects and lessons. No problem so far. I'd managed to do a few assignments while I was recuperating at home. But then she said something like, "Let's take out our writing tablets and turn to the letter J."

*Writing tablets? The letter J? What is she talking about?*

I glanced over at a classmate's desk. *Cursive writing.* The class had begun cursive writing while I was having surgery. Right then my world came crashing down. I heard in my mind a hissing message that went something like this: "Look how much they learned while you were out. You're so far behind you'll never catch up. You might as well give up now. There's no need to even try."

I sat at my desk with a lump in my throat and a pit in my stomach. I could feel the tears welling up, but who cries in class, in front of classmates? *I did.* Quietly. I tried to hide it. I felt a weight come down on my shoulders and heaviness on my brain. I felt a deep sigh somewhere within me. Years later I understood it to be, in part, a wounding. It was the message of the arrows of the enemy, aimed at my heart.[3] I didn't know what to do with those messages or feelings as a third-grader. I sat at my desk, choked back the tears and tried to form a cursive letter J.

Ground had been seized in my heart. I had received a message that would seek to inform my identity. What started out as ground taken—a beachhead, if you will—over time became occupied territory, like Simba's Uncle Scar taking over the Pride Lands.

I took *that* into my marriage, hearing messages like, "You're too far behind in love making, in cooking, in the drive to achieve, in natural talents. Too far behind your friends and their financial portfolios. Too far behind other dads and how they connect with their children. Too far behind in what masculinity entails and requires. Why don't you just admit it and give up? Why bother?

"You're too far behind Lainie too. She's ahead of you in every area. You'll never catch up to her. Why bother?"

As if marriage is not difficult enough for two emotionally healthy adults in fair weather, I had a toxic, wound-based competition going on with my wife. How do we become one when we're intent on one-upping? How do we love our wives as Christ loved the church when we have so much shame and self-hatred?

Tying the knot? How about all tied up in knots?

## Getting Help

Jesus asked the man at the pool, "Do you want to get well?" (John 5:6). I've found that he asks us the same question. Do you want to get well? Do you want to unpack your baggage?

So what did I do to deal with my baggage? (1) Our therapist helped me worked through a lot of it. (2) Lainie was there too, working on her stuff and helping me with mine. Together we learned new ways of interacting, new ways of showing our love. We learned to forgive and try again—haltingly and skittishly. (3) Our church family supported us, prayed for us, encouraged us. They gave us room to grow as we each dealt with our baggage. For five years we were part of a young-married group, a leader-couples group and a multiage community group (not all at the same time). Our friends in those groups helped us get better.

And I did two other things: (4) got help from my sister Jody and (5) took a trip to North Carolina.

Jody helped me in several ways, because she could relate to my struggles, having grown up in the same home. She had worked through a lot of her own stuff. But more than anything, she gave me permission to feel my feelings and encouraged me to express them. I had a huge amount of pent-up anger because of so much accumulated hurt.

She came out for an extended visit and spent a lot of time listening to me and validating my feelings. She helped me to *figura-*

*tively* sit some people down on the couch and say whatever I needed to say, at whatever volume was helpful. She knew I wasn't yet ready to speak with the real people, and they weren't ready to hear me. It's one thing to be angry; it's another to sin in your anger (Psalm 4:4). Jody's wise support and skillful work helped me immensely.

I was at a point in therapy when Susan said something like, "You've done a lot of good work here, but it seems something more is needed. If that's true, what might it be?" I stopped myself from giving a quick reply, knowing I needed to think about it and pray about it. Later that day, while driving and being prayerful, I had a thought about traveling back to North Carolina to visit the towns and parsonages I'd grown up in, the schools I had attended and the church buildings where my dad had pastored.

So that's what I did. I took a week-long trip back to North Carolina. Seminary classes were over for the quarter, and Christmas holidays were about three weeks away, so I had time. I bought a composition book for journaling and a camera for taking photos, packed a bag and boarded a flight to Charlotte. I planned to end up at my parents' place eventually, but I knew I first needed time with just me and Jesus. I needed to ponder and pray. Alone.

I flew back to North Carolina and set up base camp at my sister's place. Day by day I visited every town, parsonage, school and church building. I listened for the leading of my heart and let myself remember and feel the feelings. I wrote in my journal. Snapped photos. Wept. Ranted. Got it out. Took it in. I was coming to peace with themes from my past. I also fought the demonic, not only the lies that evil had heaped on me through the years, but an actual evil presence.

## Does This Stuff Matter?

The trip was a huge turning point for me. I felt almost weightless, like I could have flown back to California under my own power. The weight of my baggage had been taken off, though I was still unpacking and sorting through a lot. The trip fueled further transformation and empowered more character formation. I could now interact with others from a healthier place emotionally and spiritually. I decided to forgive and move on, to change how I related to others, including those I was called to lead.

As I dealt with my baggage, worked through my hurts and owned my culpability, I was answering the summons to live and lead with Jesus, and he was shaping my heart.

- What baggage might you be carrying?
- How might it be holding you back?
- What could you do to unpack it?
- Who could help you?

**7**

# BOSSES

## Respect Those in Authority and Use Your Authority to Serve

*You know that the rulers of the Gentiles lord it over them,*
*and their high officials exercise authority over them.*
*Not so with you.*

**Jesus in Matthew 20:25-26**

*Obey your rulers and recognize their authority.*
*They are like men standing guard over your spiritual good,*
*and they have great responsibility.*

**Hebrews 13:17 (Phillips)**

What have you learned about relating to authority figures? What do you do when you and your boss don't get along or when you *sort of* get along? When you're in charge, how do you treat those who work for you?

In my first job out of college, I worked for three years as a youth pastor in a megachurch. I was one of several pastors on staff. I kept office hours and was on the pastor-on-call rotation for people who called in or walked in needing to talk to someone. I enjoyed most of what I did with the students and our team of adult sponsors: concerts, summer camps, mission trips, retreats, weekly worship services, training leaders, hanging out, ski trips.

In addition to the good stuff of my job, I set up rooms for our weekly meetings, ran errands, filled out forms, counted offerings, purchased supplies and attended weekly staff meetings with other pastors. During those meetings, we'd go around the room, give brief updates and listen to what our boss (the senior pastor) had on his heart to share.

## Cut Off at the Knees

In one meeting, after one of our official senior-high ski trips, I gave a brief update on the trip: "We took sixty students, had a lot of fun skiing, got to know each other better, enjoyed being in the mountains, stuff like that. It was great fun being together. Didn't do anything *spiritual*."

*I had just violated a major cultural norm and didn't know it.*

What I meant was that we had a great time building community with one another, deepening relationships and enjoying God's great outdoors. I meant that we didn't have a worship service or apply any pressure to produce spiritual experiences while on the trip.

My boss sat up taller in his chair and went off on me. He reprimanded me for not doing anything spiritual on a church-sponsored activity. I felt confused, misunderstood and humiliated. I guess he saw a teachable moment. In fairness to him, yes, we could have at least led some cabin devotions. But I took issue with what he did and how he did it: he humiliated me in front of the staff.

It especially ticked me off because I was one of his most ardent supporters. Other pastors would question his decisions all the time—behind his back, of course. They'd ask undercutting questions about how he was leading the church: Don't you think it would be better if the pastor did . . . ? Can you believe he said . . . ? Can you believe he doesn't . . . ?

I stood up for him in public and private. And there he was, cutting me off at the knees. He could have spoken with me about my plans for the trip when I was making them. He could have coached me beforehand on setting up and leading what to him would have constituted a successful ski trip. (Yes, I could have gone to him and asked. But the thought didn't occur to me. I was the rookie.)

Instead, he cut me. An authority figure that I looked up to cut me.

Authority figures will cut you too, in painful places and painful ways—even the ones you respect and the ones you think respect you. It's going to hurt. You'll be tempted to harbor the hurt, take offense, get defensive, lash out or shut down. I'm not excusing what they might do. I'm trying to prepare you for the inevitable, in case it hasn't happened already.[1] They will misunderstand you. Question your intent. Power up on you. Shut you down. Look away from you when you're pouring out your heart. Try to make you fit their mold. Disappoint you.

You thought you were going to get some personal mentoring time with the managing partner of the firm. You expected the owner to take you under his wing. You thought that new assignment would be your ticket to recognition and significance—your way to gain your authority's affirmation. You assumed your mentor would be there in the trenches with you. You figured he cared about you as a person, not just a commodity. You thought he would care about your ideas and your materials, not just his own. You got cut. Hurt. Let down. But you were still expected to go into battle and to work hard.

What do you do with the hurt? How do you handle being cut by someone in authority?

## Relating to Authority Figures

God intervenes to shape our perspective on, our relation to and our use of authority.[2] God uses both painful and positive experiences to teach us how to relate to those who have authority *over us* and how to interact with those *under* our authority. What God teaches us helps us when we've been cut and can lessen how often, how deeply and how unnecessarily we cut others.

Episodes from the lives of Joseph and David teach us about relating to authority figures. The narrative in Genesis 39 picks up with Joseph's forced trip to Egypt. His jealous older brothers had sold him into slavery. In Egypt, he was purchased by Potiphar, a member of Pharaoh's personal staff and captain of the palace guard. Potiphar *owned* Joseph; he was in authority over Joseph. He put Joseph to work in his household, and God blessed the work of Joseph's mind and hands. As a result, Potiphar "gave Joseph complete administrative responsibility over everything he owned" (Genesis 39:6 NLT).

Everything except his wife. And his wife wanted Joseph: "Joseph was a strikingly handsome man. As time went on, his master's wife became infatuated with Joseph and one day said, 'Sleep with me'" (vv. 6-7, *The Message*). She kept after him day after day, pressuring him, but he continued to refuse (v. 10).

How would you have fared? The husband's at work; you're there day after day with his wife; she desires you and keeps putting pressure on you to have sex with her. Joseph *ran*. Why? He told her, "Look, with me here, my master doesn't give a second thought to anything that goes on here—he's put me in charge of everything he owns. He treats me as an equal. The only thing he hasn't turned over to me is you. You're his wife, after all! How could I violate his trust and sin against God?" (vv. 8-9 *The Message*). *Joseph saw sinning against Potiphar as a sin against God.*

In 1 Samuel 24 we learn that David was on the run from King Saul, because Saul was jealous of him and wanted to kill him. He was hiding out in the wilderness, in the hill country, in caves and mountain strongholds. His band of about six hundred men was with him. Saul, with his three thousand special troops, was in pursuit (v. 2).

Saul was chasing David, intent on taking his life. But first Saul had to "relieve himself" (v. 3). He found a cave, took off his robe and got down to business. He didn't realize that David and his men were in *that very cave.* You gotta love these Old Testament stories. They're packed with irony, plot twists, intrigue—and the outright *ordinary.* (Really, this is in the Bible.)

David's men said, "This is the day the LORD spoke of when he said to you, 'I will give your enemy into your hands for you to deal with as you wish.' Then David crept up unnoticed and cut off a corner of Saul's robe" (v. 4). David didn't take Saul's life; he cut off a piece of his robe. Then he felt guilty about it:

> Afterward, David was conscience-stricken for having cut off a corner of his robe. He said to his men, "The LORD forbid that I should do such a thing to my master, the LORD's anointed, or lay my hand on him; for he is the anointed of the LORD." With these words David sharply rebuked his men and did not allow them to attack Saul. And Saul left the cave and went his way. (vv. 5-7)

David respected Saul as God's chosen leader.

Joseph and David help us see how to relate to those in authority over us. You could argue that they lived in another time. Another place. Another culture. You're right. But I'd argue that they represent young leaders who are a part of God's greater story, serving the purposes of God in their time and place (separated by some four hundred years and in two different countries). Each was a member of the people through whom God would bless the world, and each can teach us how to relate to authority figures.

*Consider that in disrespecting those in authority over you, you might be sinning against God.* Joseph refused to sleep with Potiphar's wife, because he saw that in disrespecting Potiphar he would be sinning against God. He respected Potiphar as his human authority and God as his ultimate authority. Likewise for David, who knew that to harm Saul, his human authority, would be to sin against God, his ultimate authority.

Take your cue from Joseph and David: respect the authority figures God has put in your life. You won't always like the way they treat you. You won't always agree with their decisions. They likely will hurt you. Disappoint you. Perplex you. But you can still *respect their position.* You can learn from Joseph's and David's examples to look for God's delegated authority in the person who is over you and to submit to God's authority by submitting to that person.

## Working for a Difficult Authority Figure

But what about those cases where you've been respectful of your boss's position but have been treated poorly? Or where the conditions at work—your boss's behavior in particular—are troubling or confusing or interfering with your job performance? Here are ten strategies that might help:

*1. Remember that your boss is a person too.* Your boss has weaknesses, fears, motivations and concerns. Do you know what they are? Do you know his greatest fear? Do you know the pressure she's under? Have you taken time to get to know him or her?[3]

*2. Get to know your boss's relational style.* Find out his strengths and preferences, and then work with those in mind.[4] If he's an introvert and needs time to think about the brilliant proposals you've offered, keep that in mind. If she's an extrovert and gets excited about future possibilities but doesn't follow through on details, take that into account. Notice the time of day he functions best. Schedule discussions for that time. Find out whether she prefers setting goals and dreaming about the future or solving problems. Frame your conversation with your boss's preferences in mind.

*3. Find out if your boss is open to feedback.* If she is not known for wanting to hear what others have to say, you don't have a good chance of being heard. Ideally you discovered this when you were brought on board. Ideally the guidelines for having difficult conversations were reviewed with you as part of your orientation process. If this is not the case, find out the culture before deciding to meet with your boss. If you try to give feedback to a boss who doesn't want to hear it, you could be considered disloyal and lose your job.

*4. Think clarification instead of confrontation.* It's easier to ask questions in order to clarify an issue than it is to confront someone. Consider saying something like, "I'm confused about X and need some input from you. I need some clarification on how to address it" (or think about it). When you ask for clarification, you're owning your part in what you don't see and inviting assistance. If you go in to confront your boss, you will probably put him on the defensive.

*5. Decide whether the issue actually needs to be addressed— and when.* Maybe it does; maybe it doesn't. Maybe it can wait. How serious is the issue or condition? What kind of impact is it having on you and/or your colleagues? Decide whether your concern is a condition or a personality trait you need to tolerate and can learn from.[5]

*6. If it needs to be addressed, decide how to frame it.* Should you say, "In order to do what you've asked me to do, I need . . ." or "Here's what would be helpful for me in doing the work you've asked me to do . . ." If you can't frame it in one of these ways, is it really something you need to say? In other words, if it's not getting in the way of your mental outlook or job performance, do you need to bring it up? On the other hand, if it needs to be addressed and you're getting all kinds of signals that your boss isn't open to discussing it, you might need to decide how long you can go on working for her.

*7. Ask for permission to say it.*[6] Say something to your boss like, "I need to talk about X. Can we have that conversation? When would be a good time?" Or something like, "I have a question about X. Can we talk about that?"

*8. Speak for yourself.* Use *I* messages: "I think . . . I noticed . . . I feel . . ." Avoid *you* messages: "You always . . . You never . . . You promised . . ."

*9. Be respectful.* Your tone matters. Your gestures and facial expressions matter. Whatever you say, say it respectfully.

*10. If it's necessary, be prepared to be bold.* Tell the truth as you see it. State your needs clearly, as you see them. Remember, however, that your message could be received negatively. Be sure that you've considered your options should your message not be well received.[7]

## Using Your Authority

What about when *you're* the one *in* authority? When you're in that position, remember these words of Jesus:

> When the ten heard about this, they became indignant with James and John. Jesus called them together and said, "You know that those who are regarded as rulers of the Gentiles *lord it over them*, and their high officials exercise authority over them. *Not so with you.* Instead, whoever wants to become great among you must be your servant, and whoever wants to be first must be slave of all. For even the Son of Man did not come to be served, but to serve, and to give his life as a ransom for many." (Mark 10:41-45, italics added)

What prompted this exchange? James and John had asked Jesus for a favor. They wanted to sit at his left hand and right hand when the time came for him to enter his glory. They wanted to be right there with him, in the places of power. The ten other apostles didn't take kindly to the brazen arrogance of these two "sons of thunder." So Jesus taught them all about leadership in the kingdom—about true greatness. Notice the two key phrases: *lord it over* and *not so with you*. Jesus said true greatness is related to serving, not to being served. It is not powering up on those you lead, but empowering their growth and development, honoring their personhood. It is seeking their best. As one who leads with Jesus for the life of the world, how you exercise your authority matters. To be authorized means you've been given the right to do something, but how you exercise your authority will affect whether you're leading for the life of the world.

What's the ideal? That we use our authority to build up, not to tear down. To serve, not to be served. I wish I'd known about servant leadership when I was on a bus coming back from a youth-group ski trip in Colorado (not the one I discussed earlier). We were on our way back to Phoenix and were running late. Traffic and weather had been bad getting off the slopes. Our 11 p.m. time of arrival into Phoenix was looking more like 2 a.m., and I knew parents would be upset. If parents were upset, that meant my boss would be upset. This was not the kind of post-trip irritation I wanted to face.

When we stopped for fuel, I told the students to stay on the bus. I wanted us to get back to Phoenix as quickly as possible. Giving thirty-five-plus high schoolers time to get off the bus, get snacks, pay for them and get back on the bus would delay us by another thirty-five minutes, at least.

I got off the bus to pay for the fuel, and while I was in the gas station, I picked up a bag of chips and a soft drink. When I got back on the bus, I could feel the students' eyes stabbing me in the back. Daggers between my shoulder blades. With good reason: they were hungry too.

I felt the tension and heard the murmuring. The grumbling. They were calling me out on my double standard. One of them was Scott, Lainie's younger brother—my brother-in-law. He was one of our student leaders, and he was not afraid to share his opinion. He called me out: "Yeah, Daniel. You get off the bus and get something to eat, but not us. You're the guy in charge, is that it? What about us? What makes you so special?"

I knew then I had blown it. I had taken advantage of my position as the leader, using it to serve my own needs instead of the needs of the group. It would have been so easy to buy several bags of chips and soft drinks. That would have been serving their interests too, not just mine. But like I said, I had not yet learned the servant leadership terminology or philosophy (not that my ignorance excused my actions). Buying a bunch of snacks for everybody never entered my mind. Call me clueless.

## Leading for the Sake of Others

The central thrust of servant leadership is to use our influence to serve, not to be served. To work for the well-being of the group, for the sake of others, for the life of the world. To create cultures where people can flourish, that foster light and life. Parker Palmer writes,

> A leader is a person who has an unusual degree of power to create the conditions under which other people must live and move and have their being—conditions that can either be as illuminating as heaven or as shadowy as hell. . . . I'm not talking simply about the heads of nation states. I'm talking, for example, about a classroom teacher who has the power to create conditions under which young people must spend half their waking hours, day in and day out, five days a week. Have you ever walked into a classroom in which the leader is projecting light? Have you ever walked into a classroom in which the leader is projecting a huge and ominous shadow? That's the question. That's the choice.[8]

Servant leaders project light. They promote life through their posture and presence, through the way they bring their power (their influence) to bear and through the environments they create.

They advance God's purposes through interactions with others that elevate the human spirit.

To be sure, buying bags of chips and cans of soft drinks wouldn't have saved anybody's soul on the trip home from the ski trip, but it would have demonstrated love and respect to the students. It would have embodied for them the way of the second great commandment (love your neighbor as yourself). It would have given the students a more accurate picture of how Jesus would treat them. It would have turned on a light in the bus and in the youth group.

Sometimes, influencing others to live out the redemptive purposes of God simply means living in front of them a life of love—for God and people. It means influencing them in a loving way, through a posture that models the way we hope they'll choose to live, that persuades rather than mandates. It means reasoning with instead of requiring. It means using dialogue instead of demanding a certain way. Robert Greenleaf refers to this as a *persuasion* style of leading to distinguish it from a *positional* style. One of my mentors calls it imitation modeling. Jesus did this when he washed his disciples' feet and then instructed them to do the same (John 13:1-17). A servant leader first lives the life, then calls others to follow.

I wish I'd known about servant leadership on the way home from Colorado. Had I understood it, I could have done a better job of exercising my authority. I could have asked the students how to solve our dilemma. I could have served them in a more loving way. I wish my boss had followed this model instead of cutting me that day in the staff meeting. He could have built me up instead, while still helping me plan future trips with his expectations in mind.

- How are you relating to the authority figures in your life?
- Where might you need help?
- How does it seem others relate to you when you're the one in a position of authority?

# BLIND SPOTS

## Find Out What You're Not Seeing

*You study the Scriptures diligently because you think that in them you have eternal life. These are the very Scriptures that testify about me, yet you refuse to come to me to have life.*

**Jesus in John 5:39-40**

When we don't realize how we come across to others—how they perceive and experience us—we have a blind spot. Blind spots hinder our effectiveness in leadership, relationships and work. You won't know what they are unless someone helps you see them. You could have a blind spot like one of the following:

- *Humor.* You thought you were just being funny. Others perceived you as hurtful and insensitive.

- *Attitude.* You thought you were exuding confidence. You sounded like a know-it-all.

- *Verbosity.* You thought others would want to hear your thoughts. Perhaps they did, but you sounded condescending and you droned on and on. You bored them. They were too kind to interrupt.

- *Eye contact.* Did you know that you always look away when you talk to women? What's up with that?

- *A blunt tone.* You thought you were just being truthful and to the point. Others found you rude.

- *Answering questions.* You thought you were being helpful when you answered questions directed to your wife (or girlfriend). She—and those who posed the questions—thought you were domineering.

- *Job performance.* You believe that in some of what you do at work you're just adding your personal flair, living out the finer expressions of your personality. But people at work actually think you're trivializing the job or missing the point of what you've been assigned to do. They find your leadership difficult to follow and wonder how you've kept your job as long as you have.

- *Power.* You think you come across as sensitive and caring. Others experience you as insensitive and demanding. You don't realize how much power you project.

When I was in grad school, Dr. Gorman, one of my instructors, decided it wasn't enough to teach our course through lecture and class discussions. She wanted us to experience the content and reflect on it; she wanted us to learn by doing. Since the course was on group dynamics, she assigned us to small groups, saying we needed to determine for ourselves when we would meet, where, what type of group we would form and who would lead the sessions.

Okay, so it sounded a little like busy work to me, but I was willing to go along. She put us in groups and gave us a few minutes during the class session that day to get started. Most groups had five to seven participants. The one I was assigned to had three—like we ran out of people or something. Me and two young-adult women. The size and composition of the group felt awkward and forced to me, but it was what the instructor required, so I figured I should give it a go.

I had no idea what I was in for. No idea of the blind spot I had. You could've parked a pickup truck in it, or at least a MINI Cooper. Here came God again, with another strategy for my formation.

About five days after our initial meeting in class, we had our first group meeting. We were rotating leadership of the sessions, and I was first up to lead our mighty group of three (Sue Ellen, Kate and me). We needed to set an agenda and time frame for our meetings. I thought I was rather astute with agendas and time frames, and when I'm leading, I can be a take-charge, *let's-go*, the-agenda-is-sacred kind of leader. You know, let's get our work done; we can chitchat later. And here I was in a group with two highly relational people.

I didn't do chitchat very well; I actually had very little tolerance for it. *If we're gonna meet,* I thought, *let's have a real reason. A purpose. If we're gonna talk, let's talk about something that matters.* So as I was laying out the agenda and cranking things up for the meeting, Sue Ellen and Kate were sitting there wide-eyed and dumbfounded, wondering what planet I had just shipped in from. And they put the brakes on me. Big time. "Geez, Daniel! Is this how you lead the groups you're part of?" exclaimed Sue Ellen.

"What do you mean?" I asked.

"Like this. All fast and furious. All down-to-business. No time to check in and catch up."

*What the heck? What is she saying? I said good afternoon to each of them, called them by name, said it was good to be together, said I am looking forward to our first session. Is that not relational enough?*

I had a blind spot. Kate and Sue Ellen helped me see it.

## Do You See What I See?

A blind spot is what others can see about us that we don't see. I first learned about blind spots through the work of Joseph Luft and Harry Ingham in a consulting course I took in the early 1990s. Luft and Ingham developed a tool called the Johari Window to explain four types of self-knowledge.[1] (*Johari* is a combination of their first names.) The window is in figure 8.1.

|  | Things I Know | Things I Don't Know |
|---|---|---|
| **Things They Know** | Arena | Blind Spot |
| **Things They Don't Know** | Hidden | Mystery |

Fig. 8.1.

To read the diagram, go counterclockwise, starting in the top left quadrant. This quadrant, titled "Arena," contains information we know about ourselves and that others know about us. Here is some of my arena knowledge: my height, weight and hair color; the way I treat Lainie in public; the way I drive; some of my motives; some of my attitudes and values; some of my behaviors.

The next section down, bottom left—"Hidden"—contains information about ourselves that we know but others don't. That information is hidden to them unless we choose to share it. Here we keep our closely held hopes and longings. Or it could be where we hide our ugliest sins.

Proceed counterclockwise to the "Mystery" quadrant, which holds information that is unknown to us. Psychologists call this our unconscious self. Sometimes we get in touch with it through dreams or other means that God might use, when the time is right to reveal it to us.

The final quadrant—"Blind Spot"—holds information that others know about us but that we don't know or things we think are true about ourselves but others don't agree with. When you have a blind spot, you see and believe one thing about yourself, while others can see what you don't. These are not simple differences in preferences; they are attitudes and behaviors that hinder how you relate to others and thereby diminish your leadership effectiveness.

## Organizational Blind Spots

When we don't realize how we come across to others—how they experience us—we have an interpersonal blind spot. I had an interpersonal blind spot with my group in Dr. Gorman's course.

When we don't realize how we come across in organizations—how colleagues and constituents perceive us—we have an organizational blind spot. I had one of them in a job I had in Southern California. I was prepping for a presentation I was about to give. Here's how I thought about the presentation—and what actually transpired. I thought, *This will be my finest hour with the organization. A defining moment in my early tenure [eight months] as primary spokesperson and key leader.* I planned to challenge and inspire the troops into new territory—all 150 of them. They would see the logic and wisdom of the new direction, hear the passion in my call to action, feel the excitement of a new day dawning. Perhaps they would even stand and applaud. They would show their support for me and the bold new direction, with congratulations all around, pats on the back, hats off to the bold and visionary leader.

It didn't happen that way. People were confused. They wondered why I was the one initiating the call to action; they didn't see me as the leader at all. I was a spokesperson, maybe, but not the leader. Not the one who set the direction and led the way.

I had a lot to learn. I had an organizational blind spot. This was similar to what happened in the staff meeting when my boss unloaded on me: I had run full speed into what organizational development specialist Edgar Schein calls corporate culture.[2] Corporate culture dictates the assumptions about what we do and why; what matters and why; how we proceed, or don't; and why that matters. It dictates who is in charge and why, and how decisions are made—or not—and why. I was blind to the culture.

My talk mostly engendered the opposite of what I'd hoped. Instead of rallying the troops, I left a lot of people confused, others angry and some hurt. I was minimizing what the organization had done well, unintentionally taking potshots at team leaders who thought they were giving their best efforts. They naturally rose to the defense of their friends—and started criticizing me. The young guy. The newbie. I became the focal point for those who had a complaint of any kind with the board of directors, in part because of my organizational blind spot.

### Relational Lessons

God used this to teach me about interpersonal and organizational dynamics. I was learning *relationship insights,* which happen in interactions with others. These happen especially in leadership settings as we learn how to relate effectively with other people and the organizations we serve—or how *not* to relate with them.[3]

Why are relational insights so important? Because to lead is to influence people, and influence depends on relationships—preferably healthy relationships and respectful interactions. God will teach you, through both positive and painful lessons, how to relate to the people you lead and the organizations within which you lead.

Two things are important: that you learn the interpersonal and organizational lessons that will help you lead effectively and that you recognize that God is the chief Instructor. God was working through my group in Dr. Gorman's course. God was working through the situation in my job in Southern California. If you don't see God's activity in what you're experiencing, you could think you're just going through hard times. Or you could think people are out to get you. You could blame others without examining your own relational shortcomings.

If, however, you acknowledge that God is shaping you, teaching you through the painful and positive interactions, you can welcome God's work and partner with the transformation God seeks to bring about. In the process, you'll become a more thoughtful, compassionate and skilled leader—a person of influence. The relational insights you learn will be connected with the servant leader model. You'll rely less on mandates and more on influencing others by modeling the way for them to follow.

## Reducing Blind Spots

Want to identify your blind spots and reduce their negative impact? Try these:

- On the *interpersonal* side, ask a couple of friends to tell you what they see. You might have to persuade them to be honest with you, because they might worry about hurting your feelings. You'll have to be open to hear whatever they share, and you might get your feelings hurt, but at least you'll see what they see.

- Have a mentor interview your friends and then tell you what he or she hears. Tell your friends first about the interview. Say you want their honest input.

- Have that mentor conduct a formal 360-degree assessment for you.

- Work through a Johari Window exercise with those who know you best.

On the *organizational* side, ask colleagues to tell you what they've discovered. Have them tell you the rules they've identified for "how we do things around here." Or complete a cultural audit. Start by identifying your organization's expression of these three levels of culture:

1. *Artifacts:* the visible organizational symbols, structures and systems

2. *Espoused values:* expressed in strategies, goals and philosophies

3. *Underlying assumptions:* unwritten and often unspoken beliefs, thoughts, feelings and perceptions[4]

You'll typically find these expressions in *behaviors* like the selection and placement of furniture; the office location; the amount spent on the rental or purchase of office space (or whatever the equivalent is of office space); the artwork (or the lack thereof); the organizational charts; the dress code; the arrangement and allocation of work space (cubicles, tables in open areas, couches or stiff-back chairs); the slogans; the vision statements; the position papers; the stories that people tell; how decisions are made; and how people act when the boss is present—or absent.

From your initial observation of these categories, continue by answering the following questions. Once you have your answers, see if others validate your findings. Hold them loosely at first, then modify as needed.

- How do people generally interact with one another? What language, customs, traditions or rituals are in play?

- What are the spoken and unspoken group norms?

- What are the stated values? What are the unstated but actual values? What gets rewarded? Who gets rewarded?

- What do the formal philosophical statements, policies and procedures tell you about the "rules of the game"?

- What's the overall feeling, climate or atmosphere? The vibe?

- What skills have become sought after?

- What are the preferred mental models or worldview?

- What understandings and meanings are shared among your coworkers?

With answers to these questions, you should be more attuned to the rules of the game. More aware of potential blind spots. More alert to where you could trip yourself up.

We've all wondered of others, "Don't they see what they're doing, how they're coming across?" Sometimes they do; a lot of the time they don't. They've wondered the same thing about you.

Blind spots. We all have them—and God will shape us to see them and correct them.

- What blind spots have you discovered that you have?

- How did you discover them?

- What steps could you take to identify other blind spots?

## 9

# LOST IN TRANSITION

### Lean into Jesus in the In-Between Times

*But very truly I tell you, it is for your good that I am going away.*

**Jesus in John 16:7**

*My heart is breaking as I remember how it used to be:*
*I walked among the crowds of worshipers,*
*leading a great procession to the house of God,*
*singing for joy and giving thanks*
*amid the sound of a great celebration!*

**Psalm 42:4 (NLT)**

What do the following have in common?

- You graduate college, move to a new city and begin a new job. You might or might not like the job. You feel the loss of what was, but you know you can't go back. You miss your college friends. You try to find meaning in your new job and search out a new community to connect with. You're not really sure where you fit. New relationships don't form as readily or fit as comfortably as they did in college.

- You spend a few years at that job then move to a new city and begin grad school. You miss the friends you made in your former city. You either like the school or it doesn't turn out to be what you'd hoped. You like some of your classes but not all. You try to make new friends, but it takes a while.

- You finish grad school, move to a new city (or not) and begin a new job, a job that lets you live more fully out of your passion (what you deeply care about) and your giftedness (what you're really good at). You feel great about what your new job lets you do, and you feel excited about the challenge it brings and the opportunity to spread your wings and fly. But some of your co-workers turn out to be a pain in the neck, and your new supervisor is too preoccupied to help you get on board effectively.

So, what do these vignettes have in common? Each involves a transition. A move from the familiar to the unfamiliar. A move from the way things have been to the way they will be. A move from the old to the new. And each entails some form of loss.

### Definition

Transitions are in-between times—living in the already but the not yet. In the examples above, you've *already* graduated college, but you're *not yet* connected to your new community. Or you're in grad school, but you haven't yet found the groove in your studies or found your people. You've moved from one phase of your formation but haven't yet entered the next phase. You've gained the new, but you've lost what was. Often transitions are periods of uncertainty, and God uses them to deepen our trust in him.

When I moved from Phoenix to Pasadena, California, to

attend grad school, I went through a transition. I'd been in Phoenix three years, leading a youth ministry. I knew a lot of people, and a lot of people knew me. I felt at home in Phoenix but uprooted and out of place in Pasadena and in Southern California in general.

Outside of immediate family (Lainie and our six-month-old daughter), I knew two people in Pasadena and only two people knew me (our good friends Lance and Linda). I needed friends, a new support system. That's not a big problem if you're gregarious and outgoing. It's not a big problem if you're on top of your game and feeling confident. But I was feeling displaced, alone and lonely. Disconnected from friends and family. And cut off from the friendly and familiar. Even though I had been feeling restless in Phoenix, I didn't have to leave. I was on top of my game there. Now I wasn't even on a team. I wasn't even sure what game I was playing, except "go to grad school."

As much as I was glad to be in grad school, I was back on my heels a bit. The old tapes in my head were running constantly, on full volume: "You're not enough; you don't have what it takes; you're too far behind to excel here; you're an idiot for moving your family here" (et cetera, *ad nauseam*). We were living in a one-bedroom apartment, and money was tight. Lainie's job wouldn't begin for another four weeks. My classes wouldn't begin for another eight weeks. We had moved too soon.

## Shaped by Transitions

I didn't realize that I was in transition in my formation as a person, toward the life stage of adulthood, and in my development as a leader.[1] I also didn't realize that while transitions can unsettle you, they're also invitations to *lean in and go deeper with Jesus*.

Transitions typify life in our twenties. The majority of twenty-somethings move from one city (or cities) to another, change jobs (more than once), graduate from college or a trade school and perhaps a graduate program, and possibly marry, purchase a home and have children. The authors of *TwentySomeone* write, "The reality is, most people experience more drastic life changes in their twenties than in any other stage of life, especially when we realize that marriage and kids and career—alone or in any combination—are going to be as much or more work than we thought they would be."[2]

Given the number and nature of these life changes in the twenties, some have a "quarterlife crisis."[3] Since 2004, developmental theorists in the United States and industrialized countries have begun calling the twenties (actually eighteen to twenty-nine) a developmental life stage—the stage of "emerging adulthood." Jeffrey Jensen Arnett, who is credited with coining the term, explains that several factors have converged in the past fifty years and point to the need to recognize a new life stage:

> The rise in the ages of entering marriage and parenthood, the lengthening of higher education, and prolonged job instability during the twenties reflect the development of a new period of life for young people in the United States and other industrialized societies, lasting from the late teens through the mid- to late twenties. This period is not simply an "extended adolescence," because it is much different from adolescence, much freer from parental control, much more a period of independent exploration. Nor is it really "young adulthood," since this term implies that an early stage of adulthood has been reached, whereas most young people in their twenties have not made the transitions historically associated with adult status—especially marriage and parenthood— and many of them feel they have not yet reached adulthood. It is a new and historically unprecedented period of the life

course, so it requires a new term and a new way of thinking; I call it *emerging adulthood.*[4]

According to his research,

For today's young people, the road to adulthood is a long one. They leave home at age 18 or 19, but most do not marry, become parents, and find a long-term job until at least their late twenties. From their late teens to their late twenties they explore the possibilities available to them in love and work, and move gradually toward making enduring choices. Such freedom to explore different options is exciting, and this period is a time of high hopes and big dreams. However, it is also a time of anxiety and uncertainty, because the lives of young people are so unsettled, and many of them have no idea where their explorations will lead.[5]

Notice Arnett's language: "a time of anxiety and uncertainty . . . so unsettled." He later observes that one of the five features that typifies emerging adulthood is that it is "the age of feeling in-between, in transition."[6] That's what I felt—the age of *in-between.* Between Arizona and California, Phoenix and Pasadena; between churches and groups of friends; between jobs; between work and a graduate program. And our first child was six months old. Our life changes were all over the map.

Transitions combine this weird blend of positive and negative, of helpful and painful. While they help us grow and we must pass through them to mature, they're often experienced as loss, and losses need to be grieved. In a transition, it's common to feel the following losses:

- *Attachment.* To whom am I connected now? Who are my people?
- *Territory.* Where do I belong now?

- *Structure.* What's my role? How do I order my day and week?
- *Identity.* Who am I, really?
- *Confidence.* Do I have what it takes?
- *Future.* Where am I going?
- *Meaning.* What's the point of all this?

In Phoenix, I was connected to my immediate and extended family, who were local. I was also connected to my colleagues at work, at church and on our softball team (attachment). Phoenix was home (territory). We cheered for the Suns and the Sun Devils. We ate great Mexican food at Carlos O'Brien's, Chicago Dogs at the Great Dane Dog House and subs from Appetito's. We went tubing on the Salt River, rode the waves at Big Surf and hiked the Havasupai Canyon.

I worked at The Valley Cathedral, where I was director of youth ministries (identity). I usually worked most of Sunday and another four or five days during the week (structure). The point of it all (meaning) was to get high school students into God's presence, to help them know and love Jesus and to help them find a place to do what they were passionate about for the youth group.

I waxed and waned on how well things were going and how suited I was for the job (confidence), but that was due more to my issues than what was happening on the job. Toward the end of my tenure, I knew I was heading to grad school (future) but wasn't sure what it would be like. Now that we were in Pasadena, I felt the loss of what *had been.* I was living in the in-between.

Lainie was too. She was a new mom. She had a new job at a new school in a new city. She had new colleagues. She was a champ too, working with me to get our family settled and get ready for the start of her school year. Because we each have a sense of adventure and like to explore new places, we did a lot of half-day trips to check out the Southern California scene. Like me, she struggled at times, but having a built-in community at work and a schedule to keep every day helped her settle in quicker.

## Transitions in Leadership Formation

We were in transition in our development as young adults, but also in our *leadership formation.* A leadership formation transition is a period between two phases or subphases of development. It's something all leaders go through. It's how we get from one place in our development to another place. A transition can take as little as three months and as long as three to five years, depending on the work God wants to do in us and our response to God.

God had formed me in Phoenix by shaping my character and values, and teaching me about relationships and leadership. Now it was time for the next phase, for a new round of lessons and shaping activities.

If I'd known about transitions, I could have told myself to calm down, take one day at a time, keep moving forward. I would have leaned more into God, going deeper and learning what God wanted to teach me. I would have embraced this work that God does in leaders' lives. I could have sketched some diagrams like those in figures 9.1 and 9.2, if I had known more about leadership formation.

| **In Phoenix:** my previous phase of formation | I was here, in a **transition** between phases | **In Pasadena:** my next phase or phase of formation |

**Fig. 9.1.**

A leader's formation can be plotted along a generic timeline of development that looks something like figure 9.2. Transitions occur where phases overlap. The work of one phase is being completed while another is being initiated.[7]

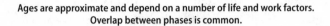

Ages are approximate and depend on a number of life and work factors.
Overlap between phases is common.

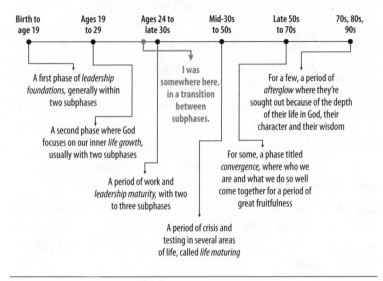

| Birth to age 19 | Ages 19 to 29 | Ages 24 to late 30s | Mid-30s to 50s | Late 50s to 70s | 70s, 80s, 90s |

A first phase of *leadership foundations,* generally within two subphases

A second phase where God focuses on our inner *life growth,* usually with two subphases

A period of work and *leadership maturity,* with two to three subphases

I was somewhere here, in a transition between subphases.

A period of crisis and testing in several areas of life, called *life maturing*

For some, a phase titled *convergence,* where who we are and what we do so well come together for a period of great fruitfulness

For a few, a period of *afterglow* where they're sought out because of the depth of their life in God, their character and their wisdom

**Fig. 9.2.**

It seems easy enough to sketch timelines and label a transition. But living through one is different. In a transition, you feel inadequate, confused, lonely and separated from God. You can't return to what was, but you're not sure what's still to come. You might have ideas and hopes for your future, but you can't see all that the future holds.

A number of leaders in the Bible went through transitions. When God began to work with them, they felt the winds of change blowing through their lives. They didn't fully see the future to which God called them. They struggled at times to step into the new work that God had for them to do and the new person that God was shaping them to become.

God made Moses the leader of the exodus and the primary figure in the formation of Israel as God's covenant people. But first God took Moses into the desert and taught him how to care for his father-in-law's sheep. The desert years were part of his transition, which ended when God appointed him to lead Israel out of Egypt.

God transitioned Joshua from being an assistant to Moses to succeeding Moses to become Israel's commander in chief. But several times God needed to tell Joshua to be strong and take courage. No wonder! Joshua got his start at the Jordan River in flood stage; his first instruction was to circumcise the entire army; and the ancient, walled-in city of Jericho was the site of his first battle.

God took David from being a shepherd of sheep and made him shepherd (king) of Israel. David was great with a slingshot, but he had to learn to dodge Saul's javelin and lived as an outlaw for years.

In the New Testament, Jesus transitioned Peter (previously named Simon) from fisherman to chief apostle and Paul from persecutor of the church to planter of new churches. And their transitions were tumultuous. On one occasion, Jesus looked at Peter and told him, "Get behind me, Satan!" (Matthew 16:23). Paul caused such an uproar through his first sermons in Damascus that his opponents plotted to murder him—then and there! His newfound friends helped him escape by lowering him in a basket over the city wall. Peter and Paul were two stalwarts of the church in the first century, yet even their transitions were bumpy and at times painful.

## Growing by Looking

Transitions can be painful, but they're greenhouses for growth. They help us grow by providing opportunities for us to

- look back and bring closure to previous experiences and lessons learned;
- broaden our outlook by learning new perspectives and making new discoveries;

- make decisions that propel us into a new phase of work and formation as a leader; and

- deepen our relationship with God.

To say it another way, we grow during transitions by taking time to *look around*. If you're in a transition, you need to look back, inside, up and ahead.

*Look back* to see where you've come from. Write down the lessons you learned about life, God, yourself, people and leadership. Open your journal, title a page "Looking Back," and write the lessons that quickly come to you. Add more lessons as you remember them.

*Look inside.* Write down what you're good at. Take note of what you care about. Write the painful stuff as well as the positive. Write when you showed up and came through. Write when you didn't. Write about what you're pleased with and what troubles you. Be honest. This might be some of the very stuff God wants to deal with during your transition.

*Look up* to God. Take note of what you see. What are the images that pop into your mind when you think of the Trinity: Father, Son and Spirit? Tell God what you see and how you feel. You don't have to sweet-talk God here. The writers of the Psalms didn't. God already knows what you think. Go ahead and have a conversation. Praise God. Plead with God. Ask your questions. Be honest.

It's likely that your image of God is something that God will shape during your transition, as well as how you relate to God. Don't be surprised if it seems that God isn't listening or if what helped you connect with God in the past doesn't seem to work any longer. To be summoned to follow Jesus is to be invited into new ways of connecting with God in different seasons of life.

Finally, *look ahead.* You'll naturally do this from the outset, because moving into a new thing is part of what the transition is all about. You'll want to look ahead *and* you'll want to get there yesterday. But you can't live there yet. The transition doesn't end just because you want to rush off into the future, to hurry up and stop the pain. Slow down.

I began grad school seeking a master's degree on a learning track titled "pre-PhD in New Testament studies." But I graduated with a general-emphasis Master of Divinity degree with an informal concentration in church development and leadership development. The pre-PhD was just one example of the future I thought I saw. I had no idea that I'd convert to an MDiv or end up dealing with so many inner-life issues. So look ahead, but hold it loosely. Spend time looking back, a bit more looking inward and a lot more looking up.

If you do these four looks, you'll grow. You'll get a lot of good out of your transition. And God will meet you in it and sustain you through it.

### Isolation

Part of what made my transition difficult was loneliness. I felt lonely and isolated because I was cut off from my former place, from my former people and from God.

*Isolation* comes from being set aside from normal leadership involvement, usually for an extended period, for God to meet us in a new or deeper way. God uses isolation to teach important lessons that we can't learn in the day-to-day pressures of typical work and leadership settings.[8]

You could experience isolation through one or more of the following:

- sickness (such as depression or an extended hospitalization)
- imprisonment (less common for Christians in Western countries)
- ongoing personality conflicts or organizational dysfunction at work
- by making a choice to step away from the routine of work for a sabbatical or some other form of renewal
- by seeking further training or education

When I moved to Pasadena, my isolation was related to the final type. God was opening the door for me to take the next step. I didn't know that I was entering a transition or that I would experience isolation, but God did. And God used that period to draw me closer and to continue shaping me as a follower and as a leader.

Sometimes the isolation is geographic. Mine was. At other times, it's more psychological or emotional. That happens when you stay in the same location and continue doing the same work, but you feel cut off from the work, distanced from those around you and far from God. In either case, the isolation is an invitation from God to press in.

My isolation broke me down. For the first several months I felt cut off from God and people. I tried to connect, but the relationships seemed to go nowhere. I went from being something of a big man on the church campus to being an unknown on the grad school campus. Lainie was flourishing at work and making friends there. I was doing the full-time dad thing a couple of days a week and getting my butt kicked in Hebrew and Greek classes.

I was in Southern Cal, so you'd think I'd have been having fun. Los Angeles was hosting the Olympics, the beach was forty-five minutes away, Dodger Stadium was only fifteen minutes away, Hollywood only thirty, and the days were always warm and sunny. But I may as well have been on the dark side of the moon. I knew I'd heard from God to move, but I hadn't heard much since moving—at least as I'd grown accustomed to hearing God speak (for example, in preparation for talks to give the youth group; in worship services I helped lead for the youth group; in prayer). Understanding that God can use other means to communicate with us is one set of lessons I learned.

In figure 9.3 are some other lessons God teaches in the different types of isolation. See if any of them ring true for you.[9]

| Type of Isolation | God Might Be Teaching |
|---|---|
| Sickness | Dependence on God for strength |
| | Insights on supernatural healing |
| | To deepen the inner life, especially intercessory prayer |
| | The urgency of the time remaining to accomplish a given task |
| Imprisonment | Dependence on God for strength |
| | To sharpen mental faculties and memory |
| | Submission to God's will |
| | To influence others through writing and/or prayer life |
| Personality Conflicts | Submission to God's will |
| | Submission to spiritual authority |
| | The value of other people's perspectives |
| | Dependence on God for perseverance |
| | How organizations actually function |
| Self-choice for Renewal | New perspectives on work and leadership |
| | To rekindle a sense of destiny |
| | The power of prayer |
| | Inner convictions from Scripture |
| | Guidance for life, work and leadership |
| Self-choice for Education | New perspectives on work and leadership |
| | To rekindle a sense of destiny |
| | Openness to new ideas and change |
| | Broadening through exposure to the insights of other people |

**Fig. 9.3.**

Transitions and isolation bring the deeper work of the "in-between times." They try your faith and stretch your soul. You'll be tempted to rush through them, to get out of them as quickly as possible, but choose to stay with them. Let God use them to do a work in your heart, to get you what you need for the next chapter of living and leading with Jesus. Ask Jesus to meet you in the waiting and to sustain you there. His work in you will bring you through to the other side with deeper humility, stronger character and greater reliance on him.

• When have you experienced a transition?

• How did it feel?

• What helped you get through it?

# PART THREE

# SENT

## Stepping Up to Lead and Serve Others

*Follow me
and I will make you
**fishers of men.***

**Jesus**

*I had not yet told them what my God had
put in my heart to do for Jerusalem.*

**Nehemiah, son of Hacaliah**

*Use whatever gift you have received to serve others,
as faithful stewards of God's grace in its various forms.*

**1 Peter 4:10**

# GETTING DIRECTION

## Seek God's Guidance

*Very truly I tell you, the Son can do nothing by himself;*
*he can do only what he sees his Father doing,*
*because whatever the Father does*
*the Son also does.*

**Jesus in John 5:19**

If we're going to work and lead with Jesus, we need to be able to recognize his voice, to hear what he wants us to do. We may need direction for the group we lead, for our business or for our family. Or we may need to know if we should accept a particular job offer. In any case, understanding where Jesus is leading us and then aligning our lives and leadership with that direction is essential to leading for the life of the world.

My introduction to this started in a worship service I attended during the first semester of my sophomore year of college. I was sitting to the side of the main auditorium in one of the overflow sections that the ushers would open for large crowds. As the guest speaker was preaching, I had a thought that seemed to be an idea for a topic for a work presentation. *Interesting,* I thought. *I should remember this.*

Round two of the lesson happened another Sunday a few weeks later. I was thinking about a presentation I was scheduled to give in a couple of weeks. I was wondering what topic, theme or points to get across. Then I had a thought pass quickly through my mind—the thought I'd had a few weeks earlier, followed by the ensuing dialogue:

"Remember? You were going to remember that."

"Oh yeah, I remember. Talk about that?"

"Yes, talk about that."

It seemed like I was hearing God and receiving direction, so I tested it. I prepared a presentation along the lines of what I'd heard and shared it with the group. They appreciated what I shared. It helped them.

## Voice Recognition

God was helping me learn to recognize God's voice. I was experiencing a *word check,* which happens when God works in our lives to sensitize us to God's voice. Word checks develop our ability to hear from God, understand what God is saying, and see God's direction worked out in our lives—either personally for ourselves or corporately with those we lead.[1]

The Old Testament leader Samuel learned as a boy to recognize God's voice (1 Samuel 3). And he grew in that capacity throughout his life. His sensitivity to God's voice was especially important for him, given his role as prophet to Israel. He would learn not only to hear God's voice—God's direction for Israel and her leaders—but also to discern whether it was truly from God. He would learn to hear God's voice by seeing it worked out in the lives of the people.

Peter experienced a word check when the Holy Spirit instructed him to go with three Gentiles to the home of a Roman centurion,

Cornelius (Acts 10). The instruction came in conjunction with a vision he saw, repeated three times, about eating clean and unclean foods. According to Jewish dietary laws, Jews were not allowed to eat with "unclean" Gentiles or to eat their unclean food. But the vision Peter saw instructed him to do just that. And when the vision was followed by the invitation from the three Gentile visitors, he understood that he should go. He knew that God was guiding him. When Peter arrived at Cornelius's home, God confirmed the instruction by sending the Spirit upon Cornelius and his family. Peter learned that Gentiles were not unclean and that Jesus would indeed send the Spirit to them.

Both Samuel and Peter responded positively to God's shaping. They then increased in their capacity to receive direction from God and to apply it to their lives and work. They became sensitive to God's voice and developed in their ability to influence others in the direction of God's purposes.

## How God Speaks

God will help you learn to recognize God's voice.[2] God speaks through circumstances, your heart, the church and the Word. God speaks through other ways than these, but these four are a good place to begin listening for guidance.

*God speaks through circumstances.* Perhaps you've heard the Christianese phrases "open doors" and "closed doors." They're based on the understanding that God speaks through circumstances to give us direction. "Open doors" can refer to circumstances where opportunities arise or something becomes available at a timely moment or the way to do something becomes clear and unhindered. "Closed doors" usually means an opportunity is blocked or something desired is not available or the way to do something is hindered or unclear. Sometimes, not always, God speaks through circumstances.

*God speaks through the heart*—through desires, convictions and feelings. God spoke to Nehemiah through his heart about the plight of Jerusalem and the need to go there to rebuild the walls and gates of the city. Nehemiah was moved by the condition of the people, because God touched his heart. He was convinced he needed to do something to alleviate their shame and disgrace (Nehemiah 1–2).

*God speaks through the church.* By this I mean decisions reached by church bodies we belong to as well as through individual Christians who've learned to walk with God. God spoke through church leaders in Acts 15 when they met to consider what to expect of Gentile Christians who were being received in local churches. God spoke through the believers in the church at Antioch in Acts 11:28-30 when they discussed how to respond to a prediction of a famine.

God speaks through tradition and the sacraments. By tradition I mean the body of wisdom and insight gathered by the church through the centuries. Throughout history, church leaders and councils have debated how God has been at work in the church, shaping her life and theology. The Nicene Creed is one example of how God speaks through the tradition of the church. Some believe that forms of worship that have endured from the first centuries of the church's history would be another example.

Water baptism and Eucharist are two sacraments through which God speaks.[3] They are visible words of what God does in our lives: cleansing, adopting, nourishing and renewing us. Through marriage, God speaks about the union of believers with Christ. Through confession, God proclaims forgiveness. When we watch or take part in the sacraments, God is "signing" to us, speaking to us in the here and now about how God sees us, thinks of us, longs for us and calls to us.

*God speaks through the Word*—both the written Word and the revelatory word. Hearing God's voice in the written Word means discerning biblical truth on a given matter. This includes truth drawn from direct teaching on a particular subject as well as principles derived from teachings and illustrations. It includes those times when we sense God speaking to us about a specific issue through the Scriptures, talking to us about how a certain Scripture or truth applies to what we're facing or going through. Sometimes it happens when we're reading Scripture and a particular verse or phrase comes alive to us, resonating with us at a deep level or providing meaning for what we're going through at that point.

A "revelatory word" involves God's direct intervention to give a specific word of direction, application or clarification on a situation. Sometimes God gives a revelatory word directly to you (through an audible voice, a dream, a vision or an angelic visitation). At other times, the revelation may come through a person with a gift of the Spirit, such as a word of knowledge, a word of wisdom, a word of faith or a prophetic insight.

## Cautions

Even though God is committed both to guide and to teach us to hear God's voice, our development of voice recognition isn't always easy. God's direction isn't always as obvious as we'd like. While we might prefer God to leave a Post-it note for us on our bathroom mirror, getting guidance doesn't generally work that way. Sometimes the lines of communication seem blurred. At other times we find ourselves choosing between two very good options. We could go left or right and still be correct. We also need to *weigh differently* each of the means through which God might speak. So let me add four points of caution here.

*God's voice in the written Word is foundational.* A revelatory word should never contradict the written Word—the consistent and particular teaching of Scripture. Revelatory words for guidance should be confirmed, especially those for major decisions. When you're seeking direction on a major life issue, get counsel from others in your community who know you, particularly those who are older and wiser. As we read in Proverbs, "plans fail for lack of counsel, but with many advisers they succeed" (15:22).

***God or the enemy can cause circumstances.*** The Spirit of God would not permit Paul to minister in Asia or Bithynia (Acts 16:6-7). On another occasion, Paul wrote that the enemy prohibited him from visiting the Christians at Thessalonica (1 Thessalonians 2:18). So major decisions should never be made on circumstances alone. When the circumstances are timely, however, and when they match up with the way you've been praying, they can boost your conviction that you're hearing from God.

***What God says to us inwardly must be tested.*** The desires of the heart can't always be trusted. It's easy to confuse what we think God is saying with what we *hope* God will say. Honor your inner convictions, but not if they violate biblical truth.

***You are responsible for your decisions.*** While you'll want to take advantage of what God has taught others in the church, remember that you alone are responsible for your decisions. Where biblical precedent supports counsel from others, take it into account. Listen to wise counsel, but others are not responsible for getting God's direction for your life.

Here's a guideline to remember: Generally, major decisions should not have any contradictions between the four ways God speaks listed above. On some decisions, there may be silence in one of the four ways, but not contradictions. If there are contradictions, wait for clarification.

## Tuning In

How might you put yourself in a listening posture? Figure 10.1 is a tool I'm a fan of, and you can process your findings with others after you do it on your own. Write the question you're facing in the middle of a sheet of paper, then draw four quadrants coming out of the central question, one for each of the different ways through which God might choose to speak. Then pray over the page and reflect on it.

Fill in each quadrant as you "hear" God's voice. If you don't hear anything in a particular quadrant, leave it blank until you do. In your early to late twenties, if you're seeking earnestly, you probably won't go longer than a few weeks without some pretty clear indications of how to proceed, unless it's a major decision point.

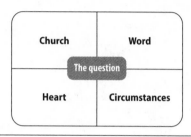

**Fig. 10.1.**

As you work through the quadrants in figure 10.1, jot down observations like these:

- What I'm hearing: _____

- Input from others: _____

- Implications: _____

Hearing from God is essential to living and leading with Jesus. God develops our capacity to recognize God's voice and then challenges us to follow—to step out and obey. First we hear the summons, then along the way we receive ongoing direction for us and for the people we lead.

- Where do you get direction for those you lead?

- In what ways do you typically receive God's guidance?

- What might God be saying now about what's next for those you're leading?

# MAKING MEANING

## Help Them See Why It Matters

*Tell them, "The kingdom of God
has come near to you."*

**Jesus in Luke 10:9**

God calls us and shapes us for relationship and partnership so we can be a positive influence in the world. We can do that on our own by serving at a soup kitchen or animal shelter, working in a community garden or sponsoring a child for summer camp (and in lots of other ways too, obviously). When we seek to influence others to join our efforts, however, we're stepping up to leadership.

For example, Adam is starting a business to improve how teachers help students learn. To succeed, he'll need to influence venture capitalists and gatekeepers in education to get on board with his vision. Todd wants his children to adopt his worldview and core values. To get there, he'll need his wife's collaboration. Together they'll need to influence their children. Travis started a campus ministry in his junior year of college. He wanted others to start the ministry with him and to help him influence college students to explore and deepen their faith in Jesus. Whether working with his team or with students, like Adam and Todd, Travis was stepping into a leadership role. For these men to get where they want to go, each needs to answer the "why" question.

### Explaining Why

*This guy's good*, I thought. It wasn't just his charisma. Not just the way he connected with his audience. Not just how Jesus seemed to be present with him. There was something more. He brought clarity and set direction, but . . . that was it! He was helping people understand where things were headed—and *why it matters*. He was answering the big questions, providing direction *and* meaning.

I was listening to a leader of a global nonprofit at a conference I was attending, and I found myself drawn to two things: *that* he gave meaning and the *meaning* he gave.[1] He answered the big questions that leaders must answer.

Effective leaders do more than call on people to perform a given task out of duty or responsibility, though there's a place for duty and responsibility. They know that people are more than cogs in a wheel or numbers on a stat sheet. They know that meaning moves people. Effective leaders, therefore, help people understand *why*: Why study a certain topic? Why treat a parent with respect? Why honor a colleague's intention? Why answer a phone call in a particular way? Why complete a service call in a certain way? Why help establish a new faith community? Why show up and participate in church services? Why advance the organization's interests, and why do the organization's interests matter? Why do become *that* kind of family, team, class, collective, guild or company? Why support *that* policy or fund *that* initiative? Why create a particular culture? They connect direction (where we're going) and meaning (why it matters).

Effective leaders traffic in meaning and hope. It could be a hope that villages will get clean water, that businesses will instill cultures that dignify and unleash the human spirit, that schools will become safer places for children and those who work in them, that people who didn't have jobs last year will get them this year, that gender oppression will end, that people will give each other the benefit of the doubt, that people will trust one another.

## Essential Questions

When I attended the conference with the leader of the global nonprofit, I was introduced to a set of "direction" categories that worked well for him and his movement. They worked well because they provided a framework within which to answer the questions that gave the group meaning and helped those within it work together. The framework created the opportunity for finding shared meaning as well as alignment in pursuit of that meaning.

I mentioned in chapter 1 that part of your calling is to lead. That means part of your calling is to get answers to the big questions, because the answers guide the work. They set the direction. You either answer the questions on your own and share them with those you're serving (so they can help you confirm or refine them), or you get the key people together and determine your answers collectively. Through the answers to the big questions, and the subsequent actions you take, you *influence* where the group is heading. You set the course and the culture for the group you seek to lead.

The answers give meaning. They inspire people. They help people see why they should care, why they should get involved, why they should give, why they should commit. *And why* they should follow your lead. Here's a great question to ask yourself: Why would people want to go there or do that with me?

When leaders fail to address the essential questions, either on their own or with a team, confusion sets in. Low morale seeps in. People get crossways. Agendas clash. Productivity declines. Why?

Because people don't see the future (where you're going), where they fit (their role) and why it matters (meaning).

Below is my list of essential questions that you (or you and a group of others) should address. When I work with clients who are seeking direction, personally or organizationally, I add other questions based on what they're leading and where they are in the lifecycle of what they're leading, but these questions will get you started on the right foot. You can take the following six below from the beginning and complete them in sequence, or you can sometimes take a more nonlinear, intuitive approach and still end up with getting great answers to each of them.

*What are we?* This is the question of identity. Is your "we" a home, a couple, a family? A group, a cause, an initiative, a movement? A church, a club, a fraternity, a collective? A for-profit business or a nonprofit service group? A Bible study? Are you in a design firm, marketing firm or communication agency? Or all three? How you identify (think "identity") yourself will imply something about your meaning. But don't trust the *implication*, which is usually *implicit*. Put it into words and pictures. Make the identity *explicit*.

Call people to what matters most: the identity and the expressed meaning. Sometimes a leader thinks people automatically know what's going on inside his or her mind and heart. People don't. You need to say it, explain it and show it. Talk about what it is and why it matters. What are you leading? Why does it matter?

*What are we supposed to do?* This is the question of mission. Some writers refer to it as purpose. Whichever word you use (*mission* or *purpose*), the answer to the question (what are we supposed to do?) sets forth the fundamental reason for your existence. Identity informs mission. For example, if you are leading a Bible study, what is the group supposed to do? Study the Bible. If you don't study the Bible, you're not a Bible study. If you're leading a prayer group, you'd better pray. But even here, where you might think everyone will understand the meaning, they might not. Help them see what your mission is and why it matters.

*Where are we going?* This is the question of vision. The answer to this question defines where you hope to arrive or what you hope to become at some point in the future. Organizations can share a common mission (for example, to change lives) but the type of organization they seek to become can vary greatly (for example, local or global, organic or corporate, traditional or innovative, inclusive or restrictive) as can the impact they hope to have on the world (eliminating disease, putting an end to human trafficking and so on).

The question of vision is one place where meaning is especially important, so . . . *why* do you want to go where you hope to go? *Why* do you want to become what you hope to become? *Why* does it matter?

*How will we get there?* If you know the identity, mission and vision (you can picture it), you can then ask this fourth question. Your answers here will come in two categories: strategy and culture. Strategy is the logic that you'll employ to achieve your mission and vision, the combination of the three to five core pieces that will work together to help you get from point A to point B. But since you could get from point A to point B by several paths, *why* did you select *that* path?

Culture, on the other hand, as you may remember from the chapter on blind spots, defines the rules of the game. It's "the way we do things around here." Make it explicit. *Articulate* your culture; don't expect people to guess what it is. Inform them, then tell them why those "rules" matter.

*What's important now?* This is the question of action—of objectives that need to be achieved this year and then in the next ninety days (or in the case of a software firm, *this week*). What plans need to be enacted? This is where noble aspirations become actual expenditures of time, energy and other resources.

*Why does all this matter?* This is the supreme question of meaning. Each of the answers to the preceding questions inform your meaning, but this question sets forth the meaning in its clearest and most unmistakable form.

When you answer questions like these, as appropriate to the initiative or work you're leading, you give people meaning and help them see why it matters for them to be involved.

## Exemplary Leader

We can learn about making meaning from a leader in Israel's history. He was a secret-service agent turned governor and community organizer: Nehemiah. Perhaps you've heard of him. If not, you can read his story in the Old Testament book that bears his name. Let me share a bit of backstory here, then show how he answered the big questions.

Nehemiah was an Israelite, but he probably was born and grew up in Persia. When we meet him, about 446 B.C., he's serving as cupbearer to the Persian king, Artaxerxes. That means he held a high-level secret-service position. At minimum he would make sure the wine to be served to the king was not poisoned. On a larger scale, he would have been involved with the entire wine production process.[2]

When Nehemiah received word from his brother, who'd recently traveled to Jerusalem, that the inhabitants of the city had fallen on difficult times and that the defenses of the city (its walls and gates) had been destroyed, he was deeply moved—so deeply that he mourned over the condition of the people and the city. In fact, he mourned and fasted and prayed for several days and nights.

During his time of prayer, God touched his heart for the people and put into his heart a specific work to do. Nehemiah sensed God's call to go to Jerusalem and restore the city's defenses—but even more, to move the people out of shame and disgrace. So he prayed for favor with the king, sought the king's permission, received it and traveled to Jerusalem to lead a massive public-works project. Then he provided leadership for the spiritual renewal of the people and put in place measures for the ongoing vitality of the work.

Nehemiah was not a prophet, not a priest, but a man who walked with God and brought positive influence to bear on behalf of the people of Jerusalem. He served courageously for the life of the world—the world God had given him to influence. He answered the big questions like this:

- *Who are we?* God's covenant people.

- *What are we doing?* Rebuilding the walls and gates of the city.

- *Why?* To provide for our defense, remove shame and disgrace, and restore our dignity.

- *How will we do this?* We'll have families work on specific sections of the wall; we'll depend on God; and we'll stay focused on the work.

- *What else are we doing?* Providing for the spiritual renewal of the people.

- *Why?* To honor God through faithfulness to God and the covenant.

- *How will we do this?* By working with Ezra the scribe-priest and a coalition of other leaders, and through a wall dedication ceremony, the public reading of the law and a covenant renewal ceremony.

Nehemiah's answers defined direction *and* focused the people. They set forth the meaning that inspired the people.

## Beyond Work

You've probably thought through these questions for your work (or questions like them), or perhaps you've been part of a team that addressed them. Fantastic! If implementation is going well, if the leaders are people of character and if you're making necessary midcourse corrections, you're probably seeing some good fruit from answering the big questions.

Now *shift the focus of the questions for a moment.* Think beyond work to other areas of life: personal, family, friends, church and/or city engagements. How would you answer the questions for these areas of your life, or the "worlds" you've been given to influence? How would you complete table 11.1?

**Table 11.1.**

|  | Personal | Family | Friends | Church/City |
|---|---|---|---|---|
| What are we? |  |  |  |  |
| What are we supposed to do? |  |  |  |  |
| Where are we going? |  |  |  |  |
| How will we get there? |  |  |  |  |
| What's important now? |  |  |  |  |
| Why does all this matter? |  |  |  |  |

Let's look at the family column for a moment. When our daughters were young, Lainie and I defined the purposes we wanted to live for as a family and the objectives we wanted to have accomplished with our daughters by the time they graduated high school. Then we took action with our purposes and objectives in mind.

The five purposes we settled on were to (1) love one another, (2) love God together, (3) keep one another safe, (4) help one another grow up, and (5) have fun together. We drew images to represent each purpose, since our youngest daughter couldn't read when we decided what our purposes would be. We used a red heart to represent love for one another, a purple heart with a crown for loving God together, a brown door for keeping one another safe, a vibrant green tree for helping one another grow up and a smiley face for having fun together. I know—not all that creative on the images. But we were intentional about implementation.

The five objectives we wanted to achieve by the time our daughters graduated high school were that they would (1) feel confident to take their next step, (2) be competent to take their next step, (3) desire to stay connected with our family, (4) be able to show people that they cared about them, and (5) follow Jesus. The objectives gave us direction with each daughter, and they mattered to us. For the most part they mattered and were meaningful to our daughters too.

We set the direction and then used it as a guide for each other and with our girls, so this included the whole family. We used it to set our calendar and to shape our budget. Otherwise it seemed like we'd just drift along, reacting to whatever came our way. I wanted to be intentional. I wanted to go somewhere good and meaningful. By answering the big questions, we defined our direction and why it mattered to us. Then we led our family in light of that direction and meaning.

### Does the Meaning Matter to You?

I've said so far that, in order to lead for the life of the world, you need answers to the big questions—for whatever effort you might lead. But answering the questions for the people and work is not enough. You must also answer them for *yourself*—why *you* do the work, why it matters to *you*. Think back to Nehemiah for a moment. He did the work because the work—and the people—mattered to *him*. He found meaning *himself* in the work he was doing.

Nehemiah and the builders completed the wall in fifty-two *days*, but he spent twelve *years* in service to God and the people of the city and region. Along the way he dealt with problems from outsiders and insiders, including worker fatigue, attacks on his character, plots to discredit and assassinate him, and other expressions of opposition and conflict. He led the work and did the work, because the work mattered to him personally.

We need to get the meaning clear at the outset, and we need to keep it clear. If it's clear now, great! But what about two years from now when that four-year graduate program has you ready to pull out your hair? Or your job has sucked the life out of you? Or you're three years into your marriage and the last two have been all bumps and bruises? What happens to meaning then?

For a lot of entrepreneurial risk takers, *continuing* to do the work poses a greater challenge than *beginning* the work. Some of that challenge is related to how you're wired; some of it's connected to how entropy sets in and to how we get distracted and lose focus over time. It can also happen when the work no longer matters to you.

## Perseverance

What will help you stay immersed in the meaning? What will help you stay fueled up for the journey or will replenish your reserves when they're becoming depleted? Take some time to reflect on leaders in the Bible and how they persevered, then make an intentional choice to finish well. To start, take a look at Joshua, Daniel and Paul.

Where do we find Joshua near the end of his life, when he's probably in his early hundreds? (Scripture says he lived 110 years.) He's holding a covenant renewal ceremony, challenging Israel to faithfully follow the Lord, who brought them out of Egypt. He's modeling the way by pledging his own faithfulness and commitment to the Lord. Here's how he puts it:

> Now fear the Lord and serve him with all faithfulness. Throw away the gods your ancestors worshiped beyond the Euphrates River and in Egypt, and serve the Lord. But if serving the Lord seems undesirable to you, then choose for yourselves this day whom you will serve, whether the gods your ancestors served beyond the Euphrates, or the gods of the

Amorites, in whose land you are living. But as for me and my household, we will serve the LORD. (Joshua 24:14-15)

After forty years of serving as Moses' apprentice, after forty years of Israel's sojourn through the desert and after leading battle after battle to take possession of the Promised Land and then settling the tribes of Israel in the land, here's Joshua, still walking and working and leading with his Lord for the life of the world. Amazing.

There's another Old Testament leader who persevered and finished well: Daniel. He was close to eighty years old when he was reading the scroll of Jeremiah the prophet and discovered that the time for Israel's exile was nearing an end. That discovery moved him to intercession. We have his prayer in chapter 9 of the book of Daniel. He was eighty *years old,* still reading the prophets and interceding for God's people and purposes. Powerful example! How will you be living when you're eighty?

Let's move to the New Testament now. Take a look at Paul. Here's what he wrote toward the end of his life:

For I am already being poured out like a drink offering, and the time for my departure is near. I have fought the good fight, I have finished the race, I have kept the faith. Now there is in store for me the crown of righteousness, which the Lord, the righteous Judge, will award to me on that day—and not only to me, but also to all who have longed for his appearing.

Do your best to come to me quickly, for Demas, because he loved this world, has deserted me and has gone to Thessalonica. Crescens has gone to Galatia, and Titus to Dalmatia. Only Luke is with me. Get Mark and bring him with you, because he is helpful to me in my ministry. I sent Tychicus to Ephesus. When you come, bring the cloak that I left with Carpus at Troas, and my scrolls, especially the parchments. (2 Timothy 4:6-13)

Paul realized his death was near. He was in prison. Martyrdom was around the corner. So, what did he do? He wrote his second letter to Timothy. In other words, Paul kept working. He wanted to prepare for the future, so he asked Timothy to bring Mark with him. This was likely John Mark, who had abandoned Paul and Barnabas on a previous ministry trip, resulting in a relational row between Paul and Barnabas (see Acts 15). Apparently Paul had mended the relationship with John Mark and saw capacity in him for co-ministry. He also wanted to keep learning, so he told Timothy to bring the books and papers.

Astonishing! Paul was doing all this reading and writing and issuing of next steps with death around the corner. He knew a strong finish was already secured (verses 6-8). He wasn't going to stop short and rest on his laurels. He was plowing ahead, undeterred. Un-be-lievable!

## Going the Distance

What could you do to persevere?

*Decide today that you* **want** *to persevere.* Make the *choice* to keep on living and leading with Jesus for the life of the world.

*Make a habit of replenishing your energy.* On a daily basis, do something that refills your tank. Take a break from work or whatever else drains you, and play an instrument, go for a walk, read a book, take a nap, paint a picture, meet a friend for coffee. Do this daily.

Then unplug weekly. Take a full day away from technology, stop multitasking and keep a sabbath. Picnic, hike, fish, ride motorbikes or mountain bikes or road bikes, work with wood or metal or concrete, race fast cars, hit a bucket of balls, go surfing or spend the day in silence and solitude. Do what you find restful and replenishing to your soul.

Once a year, vacate. Recreate. What would you do? Take a "staycation"? Have a week at the beach? In the mountains? On a river? Generally speaking, trips to visit family don't count here.[3]

*Master your moods.* Moods can distract or derail you, depending on what they are. Happy moods elevate you. Energetic moods motivate you. Do-nothing moods deflate you. Negative moods weigh you down.

Moods are emotional outlooks that usually come from thoughts. Trace a mood to its origin, and you'll generally find a thought. We have to pay attention to our thinking and tell ourselves helpful thoughts that create positive emotional energy. Researchers seem to be discovering more each day about the brain and how it works as well as how it influences what we do through our thoughts.[4] When we become mindful of our thoughts and tell ourselves the truth, when we work with the way our brains work, we can learn to master our moods instead of being mastered by them.[5]

*Work on your perspective.* By that I mean try to get a big-picture view. The big picture is what you get when you're on the top of the mountain, the sun is shining brightly, and you can see for miles in every direction. Loss of perspective is what you have in a box canyon or on the valley floor; you can't see the forest for the trees. Loss of perspective is what you get when you go through isolation and transitions. Perspective is what you get when you study the lives of leaders throughout the history of the church and see how God met them in their down times, carried them through their difficulties and brought them into joyful places.

*Keep learning.* If you don't keep learning, you'll plateau in your growth as a person and as a leader. You'll become stale. Life will pass you by. If you want to persevere, you have to maintain a learning posture.

*Continue to seek intimacy with Jesus.* No one can renew you like Jesus. Nothing can replenish you like his touch on your life. I've found that I have to discipline myself for this to happen. I have to create space intentionally where I seek to meet with Jesus. Put in space for extended time with Jesus on your sabbath day.

***Form mentoring relationships.*** Mentors can help you persevere by giving you encouragement, wisdom and perspective. They can put you in touch with timely resources that will help you stay in the game and immersed in meaning. When you adopt one or more of these seven strategies, or something like them, you can keep meaning alive for yourself and have strength to continue holding meaning up to those you lead. [6]

I've taken a look at meaning in this chapter. By answering the big questions of leadership—the who, what, why, how and what's-important-now questions—you can help those you lead find the meaning that undergirds where you hope to lead them. I've also stressed the importance of you, yourself, finding meaning in the effort you're leading. Meaning answers the why question. It gives people hope—including you, the leader.

- Where are you going?

- Why should others go there with you?

- How are you doing personally with the meaning behind what you're doing?

- How's your energy for continuing to move forward?

# PLUGGING IN

## Cry Out to God for Help

*I am the vine; you are the branches.*
*If you remain in me and I in you, you will bear much fruit;*
*apart from me you can do nothing.*

**Jesus in John 15:5**

*Then Moses said to him,*
*"If your Presence does not go with us,*
*do not send us up from here."*

**Exodus 33:15**

Getting God's direction for what we're leading is necessary, but not enough. Making meaning is necessary, but not enough. To lead the way and do the work, we need God's help, God's strength, God working in and through us. We need God's empowering presence.

This lesson reached out and grabbed me the third time I tried to preach. I bombed, but it was good for me because it drove me to my knees. I felt *so* embarrassed. I had friends and family in the audience. Lainie was there. People who knew me from childhood were there. The pressure was real, and expectations were high. The content was fine, but my delivery and presence were flat. Stunted. The whole experience was painful and humbling. I thought maybe I wasn't cut out for public speaking. What was planned for thirty minutes I burned through in five, with sweaty palms and drenched armpits. My mouth felt like cotton. My hands were shaking, my knees weak and wobbly.

My first sermon, a few weeks earlier, had gone well. The second was mediocre. This third one? Painful for me *and* the audience. The fourth one was coming up in six short hours. Time was flying. I needed help.

I was desperate.

This was one of those occasions when I sensed God's guidance on the topic, but I was still floundering. After lunch, I went looking for a place to pray—to agonize. I prayed loudly, pleading for help. "Oh, God," I groaned, "these poor people have to listen to me! And I have to endure going out there to face them. Maybe I have it all wrong. Maybe I missed your guidance. Maybe I'm not cut out for this line of work. Please help, or tonight's going to be really ugly." I got down on my knees, then my face, to ask for help.

Something happened during that prayer time. Something changed. That evening's sermon was totally different from the first three. That evening it flowed. It was full of life. I was more confident and energetic, clear-eyed and clear-minded. I was more at peace. I wouldn't give it an A—probably just a C—but it was much better than the previous disasters.

The only thing I'd done differently was cry out to God for help. My review and rehearsal of the presentation had been pretty much the same, but the results were totally different.

A famous author once wrote something like this: "When I work, I work. When I pray, God works." Did he mean that our talents don't matter? That our giftedness doesn't come into play? That our aptitude fails to engage? That our motivation mucks things up? Did he mean that prayer is some type of magic potion we can sprinkle over ourselves? That prayer can excuse our lack of preparation? That prayer is a substitute for the application of our intellect and energies? No.

He meant that, as ably and as surely as these factors might contribute, nothing took the place of God's touch on his life and work when he relied on God to empower his energy and efforts.

That evening I experienced what this author wrote about. And I learned a major leadership lesson. I didn't know at the time that it was a lesson illustrated throughout the Bible in numerous leaders' lives: the essential ingredient of leadership in God's kingdom is the powerful presence of God in the life and work of the leader. That's why I say, cry out for God's help; cry out for God's presence.

The lesson applied to Abraham—a Bedouin shepherd; Joseph— Egypt's prime minister; Joshua—Israel's commander in chief; Daniel—a trusted government administrator; and Nehemiah—the cupbearer to King Artaxerxes. These men were not prophets and priests, those we would typically think of as providing "spiritual" leadership. But they were men who served God and God's purposes. Men of influence.

The lesson applies to more than the preparation of sermons and Bible studies, worship services and youth retreats. It applies to every facet of your life and work: when revenue is down; when morale is low; when conflict is high; when you're confused and discouraged; when you have questions about your marriage and your children. Or your future. Or whether to end a relationship that you know is going nowhere. Or whether to open a new market or create a new service offering. The presence of God in your life and work makes all the difference in the fruitfulness of your life and work.

To be more specific, if we're to live and lead with Jesus for the life of the world, it will require what *we* can do—but much more. It will require *God's* presence. God's touch. Our dependence on God. Jesus put it like this: "Neither can you bear fruit unless you remain in me" (John 15:4).

So how do we get God's empowering presence, God's touch on our lives and work? Through abilities the Spirit bestows, experiences with God and getting to know God in the week-by-week fabric of our lives. Let's look at each of these three.

## Abilities from the Holy Spirit

Have you heard of these men from the Old Testament: Bezalel and Oholiab? They were artisans and craftsmen who worked with stones, metals, woods and fabrics to fashion suitable furnishings for Israel's worship of Yahweh. They also taught others to do the same kind of work. How did they get their work done? Moses tells us,

> The Lord has filled Bezalel with the Spirit of God, giving him great wisdom, ability, and expertise in all kinds of crafts. He is a master craftsman, expert in working with gold, silver, and bronze. He is skilled in engraving and mounting gemstones and in carving wood. He is a master at every craft. And the Lord has given both him and Oholiab son of Ahisamach, of the tribe of Dan, the ability to teach their skills to others. The Lord has given them special skills as engravers, designers, embroiderers in blue, purple, and scarlet thread on fine linen cloth, and weavers. They excel as craftsmen and as designers. (Exodus 35:31-35 NLT)

God was with them. God gave them the ability and special skills. Moses specifically said of Bezalel that the Lord filled him with the

Spirit of God. So these craftsmen did their work through God's empowering presence and through the abilities God bestowed.

Jesus knew the Spirit would be the supreme power enabling his followers to continue what he began. When he commissioned them to call and train others in the kingdom way of life, he said this: "Do not leave Jerusalem, but wait for the gift my Father promised. . . . In a few days you will be baptized with the Holy Spirit. . . . But you will receive power when the Holy Spirit comes on you; and you will be my witnesses" (Acts 1:4-5, 8).

When the Holy Spirit has come upon you, you will receive power. God's Spirit gives abilities for doing the work, and those abilities are a manifestation of God's presence in our lives.

## Special Experiences with God

A second way we can know God's empowering presence is through experiences with God. When I look at leaders in the Bible, I see at least three types of experiences where they received a greater sense of God's presence.

*1. Revelatory.* God chose to be revealed to a leader, and the leader received a greater awareness or experience of God's presence. Often these revelatory experiences were connected with a leader's calling or need for direction or encouragement—like Moses and the burning bush (Exodus 3–4); Elijah and God's whisper (1 Kings 19:11-13); Isaiah and the vision of the heavenly throne (Isaiah 6); Jesus and the dove that descended at his baptism (Mark 1:9-11); and Saul and his Damascus Road experience (Acts 9:1-19). Each experience of God's presence empowered the leader to take the next step—and subsequent steps—in living God's call with courage and conviction.

*2. Renewal.* In these instances, the leader was already serving God's purposes when God met him along the way and renewed his vision, strength or sense of direction. I'm thinking of David, when he and his men returned home to find that a band of marauding

Amalekites had laid waste their town and carried off their wives and children as plunder. That's when David's men thought of stoning him, but he "found strength in the LORD his God" (1 Samuel 30:6). He encountered God's renewing presence and gained strength to pursue and overtake his enemies.

***3. Rescue.*** This is divine intervention that brings deliverance. It happened at least twice in Daniel's life. Through divine intervention he was delivered from the fiery furnace and den of lions (Daniel 2; 6). It happened to Peter at least twice: when Jesus saved him from drowning after his brief walk on the water (Matthew 14:22-34) and when the angel set him free from prison and Herod's plan to execute him (Acts 12:1-24). Paul and Silas had this experience too, when they were in jail. It came in response to prayer and praise, and led to ministry breakthroughs in the city of Philippi (Acts 16:16-39) and with the jailer who was responsible for keeping them locked up, as well as with his entire family.

Experiences like these—revelatory, renewal and rescue—happen in two different ways: either God initiates them or the leader seeks them.[1] That's what I was doing in my desperation before I gave my fourth talk. I sought God. I cried out for God's presence, strength and power. I cried out for rescue.

Let me sum this up: we can't live and lead with Jesus in our own strength (nor does he expect us to). We need God's empowering presence.

God's presence is granted as God wills, through special abilities that the Spirit gives and through special experiences that God initiates. But we can also seek God's presence through special experiences, such as time away with God, days of prayer and fasting, or days of silent retreat at the beach, in a mountain cabin, in a pup tent or in a monastery or retreat center. When we do, we create space for getting to know God better through extended periods of solitude and silence.

## Cultivating Our Relationship with God

Another way to get to know God's empowering presence is in the daily fabric of our lives. We all need a consistent approach to cultivating our relationship with God. Six words can help us here: gratitude, delight, space, temperament, appointments and others (see figure 12.1).

Fig. 12. 1.

*Gratitude.* Gratitude awakens my heart and prepares me for connecting with God on a regular basis. God's many gifts are all around me. When I pause to name them and give thanks, something in me changes, opens up and reaches toward God, who has been reaching toward me. Gratitude puts me in a frame of mind and posture of heart that leads me to delight in God.

*Delight.* Notice the delight in the following verses.

- Psalm 34:8: "Taste and see that the LORD is good."

- John 17:3: "Now this is eternal life: that they know you, the only true God, and Jesus Christ, whom you have sent."

- 1 Corinthians 1:9: "God is faithful, who has called you into fellowship with his Son, Jesus Christ our Lord."

Each speaks to the possibility of delighting ourselves in God. "Taste . . . know . . . fellowship." These are expressions of delight, not drudgery. Think "get to" not "have to." Imagine hiking along mountain trails, surfing, attending air shows to watch the Blue Angels, fly fishing, river rafting, pitching a shutout or stretching out for a fingertip touchdown reception. Think shots on goal, duck hunting, rappelling rock faces and a Jason Bourne movie. John Eldredge helped me here when he wrote, "Time with God each day is not about academic study or getting through a certain amount of Scripture or any of that. It's about connecting with God. . . . The point is simply to do *whatever brings me back to my heart and the heart of God.*"[2] Whatever brings you back to your heart and God's heart? Wow! That's "get to" not "have to."

Now notice John 3:16: "For God so loved the world that he gave his one and only Son, that whoever believes in him shall not perish but have eternal life." This, too, is delight—God's delight in you. It's what makes your delight in God possible. It's God loving and knowing and delighting in you, and you loving and knowing and delighting in God. James Bryan Smith, an acclaimed author on the spiritual life, notes that followers of Jesus are, at their core, God's beloved.[3] Jesus indwells us and delights in us. That makes possible our delight in God. We cultivate our relationship with God through delight. Try that on for a while as a motive for connecting consistently with God!

*Space.* Through delight—God's for me and mine for God—I cultivate my relationship with God. Delight can strike me spontaneously, but I give it space through intention. That means I create space for connecting with God.

We bring discipline to our delight by intentionally creating space, by scheduling times and activities, relationships and experiences to express to God our delight in God and our desire to be together. If we wait for the mood to strike us, we aren't likely to grow in our delight. Over time, it may even diminish, especially as the adversary works to separate us from God. We need to discipline ourselves to create time and space to be with Jesus.

I find that I especially need to create space to engage with Scripture and to pray, which are fundamental to my communion with God. They're fundamental spiritual disciplines. They're like food and water, sleep and oxygen—essentials for deepening my love relationship with the Trinity. I *need* them in order to survive.

*Scripture.* This can take various forms, and I've experimented with a number of them: Bible study; Scripture memorization; a slow, thoughtful, devotional method of reading called *lectio divina*; using a lectionary for daily reading selections; reciting the Lord's Prayer; praying the daily offices (morning, noon and evening prayer); practicing listening prayer; or sitting quietly with Jesus for twenty minutes each day, as Pope John Paul II began to practice early in his ministry.

Engaging with Jesus through the Scriptures is how we renew our minds (Romans 12:2). It's one of the ways we build ourselves up in our faith (Jude 1:20). It's also one of the primary means that God uses to shape and equip us for the work God gives us to do: "All Scripture is inspired by God and is useful to teach us what is true and to make us realize what is wrong in our lives. It corrects us when we are wrong and teaches us to do what is right. God uses it to prepare and equip his people to do every good work" (2 Timothy 3:16-17 NLT).

When we work God's words into our life, when we base our life on God's words, we gain a sure and firm foundation for living, according to Jesus (Matthew 7:24-25). When we fail to do so, we build a life that will fall with a terrible crash when adversity strikes (vv. 26-27).

*Prayer.* This fundamental space-maker is one of the ways we speak to God and hear from God. We can present requests when we pray: "Each morning I bring my requests to you and wait expectantly" (Psalm 5:3 NLT). When we talk to God honestly, stating what we're troubled by and thankful for, prayer also becomes a means of receiving God's peace (Philippians 4:6-7). Scripture and prayer are fundamental disciplines. They are basic building blocks for connecting with God.

Other disciplines can also be helpful, either as regular features of fostering our friendship with Jesus or as occasional extras, based on our need and season of life. In the same way that switching up fitness routines can keep our workouts fresh and invigorate our physical development, taking up new ways of connecting with God can enliven and strengthen our friendship with God. Some other exercises to practice, either on your own or with a group of friends, include fasting, journaling, solitude, sabbaticals, keeping vigil, taking a retreat and going on a pilgrimage.

Silence—times set apart to be free from noise and the need to speak—provides space for listening to the still small voice (1 Kings 19:12). My spiritual director in Knoxville, Tennessee, takes men away once each month for twenty-four-hour silent retreats. Those who've gone with him have found that God meets them in the silence. By turning down the volume of their outside world, they turn up the volume of their interior life. Less noise makes for a clearer connection.

**Temperament.** Because of how we're wired, some ways of connecting with God are easier for us to access than others, seem to bear more fruit than others and are more enjoyable than others— not that we have to enjoy something for it to do us a lot of good. Using a basic temperament framework, *thinkers* might be drawn to study, *feelers* to expressive types of prayer and worship and *doers* to acts of service.

You can find resources that help you understand how to connect with God based on your Myers-Briggs temperament type.[4] You can also find resources to help you discover what my friend Myra calls your "God-language"—your heart's way of preferring to connect with God. Through her research, she's found that some of us feel more dialed in to God through nature—the great outdoors—while others connect through sacred images and art, such as icons and candles, incense and stained-glass windows. Still others are enthusiasts. I grew up with a lot of them; they feel closest to God through expressive praise and worship.[5]

Whatever your God-language, Myra argues, you'll feel more alive in God and connected with God when you're engaging through your God-language. You can explore the other God-languages and experiment with them, and even learn to appreciate them and those who "speak" them, but doing what makes your heart sing is one way that you'll deepen your experience of delight and be more likely to discipline yourself.

But let me be honest. I still struggle to cultivate my relationship with God consistently.

In spite of gratitude, which stirs my heart and helps me immensely, and delight, which I find much more life-giving than duty; in spite of thinking about my "time with God" as creating space to be together; and regardless of connecting through my preferred temperament or God-language, I still struggle. Maybe it's something inside me. Maybe it's the sin of sloth. Maybe it's forces that oppose me. It's probably a combination. I wish I were more disciplined. I wish the connecting were more tangible or consistently exciting. But most often it's not. Most often the connecting is like my dinner from two nights ago: I can't remember what it was, but it got me through the night.

I say all this because I don't want to mislead you. I don't want you to think that simply by implementing my first four words, connecting with God will be easier. It could be richer, yes, but not necessarily easier. That's one reason I add two more words: *appointments* and *others*.

***Appointments.*** Appointments are just that: blocks of time on certain days for certain activities. I make an appointment to create space to meet with God during the day. I make an appointment to worship with my community. I make an appointment to observe a sabbath day each week. I usually get away to be silent and alone with God for one to three days at least three times each year. Knowing that I have these appointments helps me put my first four words into practice. But something else helps me too: o*ther people*.

**Others.** I find a deeper texture and richness to my times of meeting with God when I do it with my allies. I need the personal time that I take to reflect and seek God, but I also need the *together* time. I need to meet with others to pray and to listen and to read the Scriptures in their presence. I need to pray for them; I need them to pray for me. Being together enlivens and enriches the experience.

## And Then?

As you draw near to God and as God draws near to you, you'll notice a difference in your life, work and leadership. Others will notice too. They'll notice because *you* will be changing. Over time you'll grow more peaceful, settled and loving.

They'll also notice because God will have granted you God's empowering presence. They'll sense God with you, God working through you. They might not call it that, but they'll notice that something is different, more settled, more robust.

Life and work might not be easier. You won't automatically hit your quota at work or have that quarter's best numbers, but you'll become more Christlike. More loving. More gracious.

But again, we don't draw near to God to get noticed; we draw near because we're desperate—and then because of love and delight. And out of discipline we deepen the love relationship.

- When did you last sense your need for God's presence?
- How did you respond?
- How do you typically seek fellowship with God?

# FIGHTING BACK

## War Is at Your Door; Stand Up and Fight

*"Be quiet!" Jesus said sternly. "Come out of him!"*
*Then the demon threw the man down before*
*them all and came out without injuring him.*

**Luke 4:35**

*Damn it, Maverick! Engage!*

**Stinger to Maverick in *Top Gun***

As you step up to living and leading with Jesus, you'll find yourself caught in a fight of spiritual origins. As you seek to bring life where you live and work and serve, you'll run into the schemes of the thief, who comes to steal, kill and destroy (John 10:10). As Eugene Peterson puts it in his translation of Ephesians 6:10-12:

> God is strong, and he wants you strong. So take everything the Master has set out for you, well-made weapons of the best

materials. And put them to use so you will be able to stand up to everything the Devil throws your way. This is no afternoon athletic contest that we'll walk away from and forget about in a couple of hours. This is for keeps, a life-or-death fight to the finish against the Devil and all his angels. (*The Message*)

I was serving at a summer senior-high church camp when I first experienced warfare with the dark side. We were holding camp at Purgatory Ski Resort, about fifteen miles north of Durango, Colorado, lodging at the Angelhaus Condominiums—six to eight campers per unit. We did morning Bible studies and evening worship services at the lodge halfway up the mountain. And we did fun stuff each afternoon, like rafting the Animas River, jeep tours up Engineer Mountain and alpine slides.

This was the summer after my sophomore year of college. I was a high-octane twenty-year-old with two years of college under my belt and fresh off a year of having surrendered to God at the Fort Lauderdale bridge. I was interning for the summer, heading up junior-high ministry but serving as a camp counselor for the senior-high students in the breathtaking beauty of the San Juan Mountains of southwestern Colorado. Talk about loving Jesus and living large!

One day at camp, I heard a knock on my door. It was Wendell, the youth pastor, the head honcho, the dude in charge. Students loved Wendell. He was the man. I was honored to be serving with him. "We're running low on supplies," he said. "So I'm heading into Durango to get what we need. I need you to hold down the fort while I'm gone. Should be back in a couple hours or so. You good with that?"

"Sure thing. Got it," I replied.

Wendell took most of the other adult sponsors into town. This was before cell phones, even the big, clunky kind. Way before texting.

About an hour later, I heard a second knock at my door. This time it was one of the campers, looking all wide-eyed and frantic.

"Daniel [voice pitch rising], can you please come to our room and pray for Clara? She says she saw a demon staring at her in the mirror of our bedroom dresser, and now she's like catatonic on the bed. And we're all freaked."

Right then I felt more like a deer in the headlights than a guy in charge and living large. I'm totally sure that's how I looked too. "Uh, sure, give me a minute. What room number?" I answered.

A few minutes later, I entered the campers' room. It was all eerie, like the electricity was working at two-thirds power, like there was some kind of mist in the air. A couple of students were on their knees, praying quietly. I had no idea what to do, so I knelt and started praying too. Quietly.

About five minutes later, the door to the room opened and in walked the morning Bible-study teacher—one of the pastors from the church. I had no idea he was around. *Thank God!* I thought. *A professional, somebody with experience. He'll know what to do. He can handle this.*

I closed my eyes and got back to my quiet prayer. When I opened my eyes a couple of minutes later, he was walking out the door. *Leaving* the room.

That's when I heard a thought that went something like this: "No, you're going to handle this. You're going to go into that room and tell that evil spirit to leave." As I was "hearing" this, I noticed that I was standing up. Yeah. Noticed. It was not intentional. But I was standing up, and as I was, I got an impression that the evil spirit was sitting on top of a chest of drawers in one of the bedrooms (not the one Clara was in).

(Yes, this probably sounds really weird, especially if it's never happened to you.)

I slowly moved toward the bedroom door and heard this instruction in my mind: "Do not be defeated." As I prepared to walk through the doorway, I encountered what felt like an invisible force field blocking my entrance to the room. I put my hands on the doorframe. I heard again, "Do not be defeated."

All I knew to do was pray in the Spirit—what Pentecostals call your prayer language (1 Corinthians 14:1-25). So I started praying in the Spirit and somehow pushed through the force field and into the bedroom. I started pointing at the space on top of the chest of drawers, praying . . . praying louder . . . and it felt like my legs were being corkscrewed into the floor . . . and like I was having one of those dreams where you try to talk and your words are all garbled and sound like they're playing on low speed on an LP turntable.

"Don't be defeated" came strong and solid in my ears, encouraging me. So I pressed on. It seemed like five minutes of pointing and shouting and praying in the Spirit. Swinging my arms. Telling that evil spirit, "Out! In the name of Jesus, get out of here!"

Then, just like that (finger snap), peace. Quiet. No more corkscrew feeling. No more garbled dream speech. It was still a bit eerie, but peaceful—like the lights had come up full strength. The mist was gone. I figured the evil spirit had left the room.

Once the bedroom was clear, I went into the other bedroom with some of the other campers and prayed with Clara. She was totally freaked by the face she'd seen staring at her in the mirror, but she was making a nice recovery, and she'd be fine.

## Combat of a Spiritual Nature

Here's how I understand what happened. As I entered that condo bedroom to confront the enemy, I was aware of stories in the New Testament where Jesus and the apostles confronted evil spirits. They were in the back of my mind. I had read the story of Jesus and the Gerasene demoniac, in which the evil spirit said to Jesus that its name was "Legion, . . . for we are many" (Mark 5:9). Whether many or few, Jesus was able to deal with it/them. He set the man free, restored him to his right mind and commissioned him to tell others what had happened to him.

I had also read the story of Paul and the fortune-telling spirit in the slave girl (Acts 16:16-40). After days of interference from the evil spirit/slave girl, Paul finally had enough, rebuked the spirit and sent it out of the girl. He set her free, but it made her owners angry. They'd been making a handsome income off her. They started a riot that ended up with Paul and Silas being thrown into prison. God broke them out of prison with an early-morning earthquake.

Because of Bible stories like these, I knew that warfare of a spiritual nature occurred in the life of Jesus and the apostles. Because of what happened in the condo, however, I learned experientially that it *still* existed. Yes, even today we fight battles of a spiritual origin.

God intervened in my life that evening to teach me about the reality of the unseen world, of evil spirits and their antagonism toward those who seek to live and lead with Jesus.[1] That was my first experience against power of a spiritual nature. It was my introduction to spiritual warfare, to battling the dark side.

Paul wrote in Ephesians 2 that followers of Jesus are engaged in a battle against the flesh, the world and the devil. I didn't fight the devil that evening. But I'm pretty sure it was one of the devil's underlings. This was my first encounter with the demonic; it wouldn't be my last.

But to reference Ephesians 2 again, sometimes our fight will be against world systems and philosophies (many commentators trace the origin of these systems to the demonic), sometimes against our own sinful human nature and other times against the "devil," what Paul refers to in Ephesians 6 as spiritual forces of wickedness.

I want to acknowledge the reality of spiritual warfare *and* sound a word of caution. When it comes to spiritual warfare, we can err by adopting one of two extremes. In his preface to *The Screwtape Letters*, C. S. Lewis puts it like this: "There are two equal and opposite errors into which our race can fall about the devils. One is to disbelieve in their existence. The other is to believe, and to feel an excessive and unhealthy interest in them. They themselves are equally pleased by both errors and hail a materialist or a magician with the same delight."[2]

The first extreme is to deny that evil spirits exist. This denial flies in the face of the biblical record as well as reports from followers of Jesus around the world today. The second extreme is to label *all* the opposition and struggles we face as spiritual warfare. As is often the case, the truth lies somewhere between the extremes. We need discernment to know the source of the opposition. Needing discernment is another reason that we need God's presence in our lives—and the companionship of brothers and spiritual fathers on the journey with us.

## Know Your Enemy

How do we know if we're up against warfare of a spiritual origin? By recognizing the tactics of the enemy. I've come to recognize opposition as having a spiritual-warfare source if it includes temptation or accusation, or if it seeks to separate me from Jesus or my fellow followers of Jesus.

The first time we see opposition to God's plans is in the garden of Eden. The opposition is subtle but deadly, seeking to separate Adam and Eve from God. The questions the serpent poses drive a wedge of doubt between the first couple and their Creator. He tempts them to ignore the boundaries that God has set, tempts them by accusing God: "'You will not certainly die!' the serpent said to the woman. 'For God knows that when you eat from it your eyes will be opened, and you will be like God, knowing good and evil.'" (Genesis 3:4-5). What's happening here? Temptation and accusation that lead to separation. It was subtle and deadly.

That's Genesis 3, in the beginning of God's story. Now take a look at the beginning of Jesus' ministry. He's just been baptized by John, the Spirit has descended upon him, which calls to mind Old Testament leaders being anointed and empowered by the Spirit, and his Father has affirmed him with these words: "This is my Son, whom I love; with him I am well pleased" (Matthew 3:17).

The Spirit then led Jesus into the desert, where he was tempted by the devil (Matthew 4:1-11). Jesus fasted and prayed for forty days and nights. Then the devil appeared. He started with an innuendo: "If you are the Son of God." Each temptation was intended to separate him from his divinely ordered mission to humankind. And Jesus used Scripture to refute and resist the tempter.

In Job 1–2, the enemy is called Satan and the accuser. He accuses God and Job. Take a look at Zechariah 3:1. There he's also called the accuser, this time of Joshua the high priest. And this time God rebukes the accuser. Read Revelation 12, and notice that in verse 10 the enemy accuses God's people "*day and night.*"

If you're being accused in your mind or if you're noticing that God and others are being accused in your mind or if your thoughts are trying to separate you from God and those you love, chances are it's spiritual warfare. It might sound something like this: "It's too late for you; you're too far behind; you'll never catch up." Or "God could not possibly forgive what you just did. This time you've gone too far." Or "God made this happen to punish you. You can't trust God. You're all alone, and God doesn't care." Or "She thinks you're a jerk. A slob. You'll never be able to please her. Never be able to live up to her standards. Can you believe she treated you that way?!" One writer refers to this as the enemy "constantly putting his spin on things."[3]

Notice that temptation often follows accusation. The temptation to give up and stop short follows the accusation that you're too far behind. The temptation to bail on your relationship with God follows the accusation that you can't trust God. The temptation to distance yourself from your wife follows the accusation that she thinks you're a jerk.

Accusation. Temptation. Separation. These aren't the only tactics the enemy uses, but they are common and can be deadly.

Spiritual warfare is serious. Jesus tells Peter that Satan has asked to "sift all of you as wheat" (Luke 22:31). The tempter/accuser asked to take the apostles and ravage their lives. To take them out before they got started on their mission.

## Worth Fighting For

I've had to fight for a lot in my life. Still do. What have I had to fight for? My marriage. My family. My faith. My mental well-being. A biblical image of God. A biblical view of myself. Strength to stay engaged in the fight. Strength to continue doing what I believe God has called me to do. Ideologies that the world system tries to impose on me (Consumerism: You are what you buy. Materialism: You are what you own. Humanism: You have within yourself all the power you need to live a life that counts.). At times, I battle my sinful human nature, holding on to hurts and grudges, seeking my own way, wanting to control life myself. On other occasions, I fight against spiritual forces that threaten to take me out through temptation and accusation.

The battles have not been easy but the causes have been worth it, and the struggles have made me stronger.

## How to Fight

When you find you're in a battle, how should you fight? Here's something I've found helpful. When you're fighting the flesh (your sinful human nature), crucify it. When you're fighting the world, renew your mind. When you're fighting the devil, Scripture says to *resist* him.

Since I'm not writing an entire book on spiritual warfare and all the strategies you could employ to fight these kind of battles, let's take a look at this one key phrase: "resist him."

- Paul writes, "Therefore take up the whole armor of God, so that you may be able to withstand on that evil day, and having done everything, to stand firm" (Ephesians 6:13 NRSV).

- James writes: "Therefore submit to God. Resist the devil, and he will flee from you. Draw near to God, and he will draw near to you. Cleanse your hands, you sinners, and purify your hearts, you double-minded." (James 4:7-8 NKJV).

- And here's Peter: "Your enemy the devil prowls around like a roaring lion looking for someone to devour. Resist him, standing firm in the faith" (1 Peter 5:8-9).

Look at these words from Paul, James and Peter: *withstand*, *resist* and *resist*. Each is from a Greek word that means to *oppose* or stand up *against*. It means to stand your ground, which reminds me of a rugby scrum. It's a strong word. In English usage, it means to withstand the action of or to ignore the attraction of. I doubt that contributors to dictionaries had Paul, James and Peter in mind when they defined the word *resist*. But it seems like they did.

To withstand the action of, to ignore the attraction of—these are powerful images.

And how do we resist? By following Jesus' example and quoting Scripture that applies to the point of conflict (Matthew 4:4, 7, 10). If we factor in what Paul wrote, we use every means God has given us: truth, righteousness, readiness, faith, salvation, the Word of God and prayer. We *use* them. We resist by bringing them to bear on the temptation or accusation at hand.

One of the early Desert Fathers, St. Anthony, did this. When confronted by demons that appeared to him claiming to bring him light, Anthony said, "But I closed my eyes and prayed. Immediately the light of the wicked ones was quenched. . . . Once they shook the cell with an earthquake, but I continued praying with unshaken heart."[4] St. Anthony also wrote of singing psalms, quoting Scripture and speaking the name of Christ against the enemy.[5]

Peter says to resist the devil by standing firm in your faith. I take that to mean stating and restating what the Bible's great story teaches us about life and God and people, and about the way things are, how they got that way, what the solution is and what our role is in the ongoing drama. We state and restate who Jesus is, what Jesus did and does, and what Jesus said and is saying to us now, by the Spirit. St. Anthony encourages us to stand firm in our faith when he writes, "Let us consider in our souls that the Lord who is with us put the evil spirits to flight and broke their power. Let us consider and take to heart that while the Lord is with us, our foes can do us no harm."[6]

When the fight comes to you, go to it. Stand up and engage the battle, leading for the life of those God has called you to serve. Fight for their freedom—and yours.

- What's worth fighting for in your life?

- When have you experienced a battle of a spiritual nature?

- How's the battle going?

# 14

# TEAMING UP

## Work With and on Behalf of the Women in Your Life

*The Twelve were with him, and also some women
who had been cured of evil spirits and diseases. . . .
These women were helping to support them
out of their own means.*

**Luke 8:1-3**

*I commend to you our sister Phoebe,
a deacon of the church in Cenchrea. I ask you
to receive her in the Lord in a way worthy of his people
and to give her any help she may need from you,
for she has been the benefactor of
many people, including me.*

**Romans 16:1-2**

Have you heard any of the following comments, or comments like them?

- She always gets so emotional. Why does she have to fall apart or blow up every time we don't see eye to eye?

- She doesn't realize that I'm the head of the home, not her.

- I spend fifty or sixty hours a week providing for our family and then she wants me to do all this other stuff when I get home.

- I help out a lot around the house. Why can't she see that?

- Well, sure, she can teach that women's class at church. That's fine. Serving on a leadership team? No way.

- Put a photo of a hot woman with it; that'll get their attention.

- Dude, yeah, that babe's really hot. You should definitely go for it.

What's beneath these comments? Is it that we

- don't understand the inherent dignity of "woman"?

- don't honor the differences between the two sexes?

- think that our job at home is primarily to provide financially?

- think that home and family are where we just help out with stuff?

- believe there's a passage of Scripture that forbids women serving in leadership roles in the church?

- see women primarily as sexual objects?

Is that what we're really saying? If so, we've got a long way to go and a lot of work to do.

## Divine Image—Divine Spirit

If we're committed to living and leading with Jesus, we need to be serious about honoring, supporting and empowering the women in our lives. It's time to see, name, create space for and call forth their dignity, capacity and destiny as our fellow image-bearers and culture-creators.

How do we do that? We start by anchoring our view of women in Genesis 1 and Acts 2. According to the creation account of Genesis 1:26-28, male and female were created in the image of God. That's a high view of male and female. *Each gender* bears the image of God. *Together* we bear that image more fully. Part of the expression of the image of the Three in One who work together ("Let us make . . . ," v. 26) is that the man and woman work *together* to fulfill the cultural mandate. *Together* they are fruitful and steward God's good creation. As Old Testament scholar Ellen F. Davis puts it: "God's dream for the human is that woman and man should be equal and complementary, for they are equally created as 'the image of God' (Genesis 1:27)."[1]

Roll the tape forward to the Day of Pentecost (Acts 2). The Spirit had been poured out on 120 followers of Jesus. They were out in the streets, declaring the wonders of God in languages they hadn't learned to speak. What was that all about? According to Peter's explanation, it was the fulfillment of Joel's prophecy: "And afterward, I will pour out my Spirit on all people. Your sons and daughters will prophesy. . . . Even on my servants, both men and women, I will pour out my Spirit in those days" (Joel 2:28-29).

Joel envisioned a time when the Spirit would be given to all God's people, regardless of age or gender. That day arrived, explained Peter, on the Day of Pentecost. He pointed to Jesus as the source of that great outpouring (Acts 2:33), an outpouring that would enable men and women to work side by side in the "last days" (the era inaugurated when Jesus poured out the Spirit and in which we now live). Because of that outpouring, Peter said, sons *and* daughters, men *and* women would prophesy as the Spirit empowered them.

That woman you're dating or have married or who works two cubicles over from you or who volunteers on that committee with you or who's been forced into prostitution, being exploited because "sex sells"—she *reflects the divine image.* And if she's one of God's redeemed daughters, she's a vessel indwelled by the divine Spirit. She's created in God's image and indwelled by God's Spirit, so why would anyone want to "put her in her place"? Would you want to settle for seeing her as someone you're simply to provide for financially or help out around the house? Or as someone you want to lust after over lunch at Hooters or Twin Peaks? Do you think that since you're the head of the home, you should be able to impose your will on her? Not if you want to live and lead with Jesus.

## Taking Our Cues from Jesus

Jesus treated women well. He reached into their male-dominated culture and lifted them up. Elevated them. How? First, he actively *cared* about women and their struggles. He healed sick women, in particular the woman who had suffered for so long with a blood disorder (Mark 5:25-34) and the woman who suffered for years from a spirit that crippled her (Luke 13:10-13). He stepped outside his primary vocation to the people of Israel to respond to the appeal of the Syrophoenician woman by casting out the demon that troubled her daughter (Mark 7:24-30). He gave back to the widow her son who had died (Luke 7:11-15). Hours from his death, his mother was on his mind, and he entrusted her care to the apostle John (John 19:26-27).

Second, Jesus brought them good news. He addressed women, not just men. He taught women, not just men (the norm among the rabbis of his day). Note his encounter with the woman of Samaria in John 4. What a scandal for Jesus to engage in conversation with a Samaritan, much less a woman who had been married multiple times! We're too far removed from first-century Jewish culture to understand just how radical Jesus was when he engaged this woman in dialogue and ministry.

Part of the good news Jesus brought was his pronouncement of forgiveness for sin, as he did with the former prostitute who anointed his feet with her tears and dried them with her hair (Luke 7:36-48). Another part of the good news he brought was release from condemnation as he did with the woman (where was the man?) caught committing adultery (John 8:11). And what good news it must have been for the woman who was chastised for pouring expensive oil over Jesus' feet when he turned the tables on her accusers and rebuked them for their attitude. "'Leave her alone,' said Jesus. 'Why are you bothering her? She has done a beautiful thing to me'" (Mark 14:6). He might be saying these very words in a lot of places today: Leave her alone. Why are you bothering her?

Third, Jesus entrusted women to be witnesses to his resurrection (Matthew 28; Mark 16; John 20) and welcomed them among his disciples. He welcomed Mary Magdalene, Susanna, Joanna "and many others" into his group of traveling disciples (Luke 8:1-3):

> The Twelve were with him, and also some women who had been healed of evil spirits and diseases: Mary (called Magdalene) from whom seven demons had come out; Joanna, the wife of Chuza, the manager of Herod's household; Susanna; and many others. These women were helping to support them out of their own means.

*Wait! What?* Mary, Joanna, Susanna and *many other women* were traveling with Jesus and helping support him and his crew *with their own money*? And Joanna was married to the manager of King Herod's household? How can we read Scriptures like these and still seek to "put women in their place" in the church? Do we think our theology justifies it? How is that posture even on the same planet with the way Jesus treated women?

Then there's Luke 10:38-42, where Martha invited Jesus into her home. Her sister Mary was there. Martha felt the pressure to host and feed those who were with Jesus, but Mary "sat at the Lord's feet listening to what he said" (v. 39). Luke went on to say that Martha was distracted by the serving that needed to take place. She was frustrated that Mary was not helping her. But when she complained about it to Jesus, he replied, "Mary has chosen what is better, and it will not be taken away from her" (v. 42).

Some commentators see Mary choosing a place of intimacy with the Lord. They use the text to call us also to practice intimacy (quiet times, a devotional life) with Jesus. That's fine, as far as it goes. But I'm pretty sure Luke did not have "quiet times" in mind (as helpful as they are). He painted a much more radical picture, showing us that Jesus welcomed the women who would sit at his feet, in the posture of a disciple. As New Testament scholar N. T. Wright put it: "The real problem between Martha and Mary wasn't the workload that Martha had in the kitchen. That, no doubt, was real enough. . . . Mary has quietly taken her place as a would-be teacher and preacher of the kingdom of God. Jesus affirms her right to do so."[2]

## Women Served in First-Century Christian Communities

Some first-century Christians picked up on Jesus' example. Men and women worked together in Christian communities that sprung up around the Mediterranean Sea. According to references in Acts, 1 Corinthians and Romans, we know that women hosted local churches in their homes, taught those who needed it, spoke God's timely words and served as deacons. It's possible that at least one also served as an apostle.[3] Take the following, for example:

*Lydia.* Lydia was Paul's first convert to Christ in Philippi (Acts 16:11-15). She was the woman merchant he met on a sabbath day along the banks of the river in Philippi. She hosted Paul and his band in her home, helping them establish the church at Philippi.

*Priscilla.* Priscilla was one of Paul's "fellow workers." Together she and her husband, Aquila, hosted a Christian community that met in their home (probably as its leaders). She was apparently such an accomplished teacher that even Apollos, a skilled orator, received and profited from her instruction (Romans 16:3-5; Acts 18:26-27). Her name is usually listed first when she and her husband are mentioned, an order that gives greater honor to the first person named.

*Philip's daughters.* The four daughters of Philip the evangelist prophesied (Acts 21:8-9), as did other women in the Christian community in Corinth (1 Corinthians 11:5).

*Phoebe and others in Romans 16.* Phoebe served as a deacon in the Christian community at Cenchrea. Paul commended her first in his list of greetings in Romans 16:1-3. Some New Testament scholars believe that Junias, mentioned by Paul in Romans 16:7, was an apostle. Others say she was *esteemed*, along with Andronicus, *by* the apostles. Paul also singled out Tryphena and Tryphosa, "those women who work hard in the Lord" and his "dear friend Persis, another woman who has worked very hard in the Lord" (v. 12). These are but a few of the women Paul recognized for their work and friendship.

Stop! Read that last sentence again. Paul named, called out, affirmed and honored these women by name for their work in the Lord. Their work *with* him. Like Jesus, Paul elevated their status.

## Guiding Principle #1

When I read Genesis 1 and Acts 2 and reflect on how Jesus and Paul related to women, I come away with a guiding principle for my work with them: different strengths (Genesis 1) but equal partners (Genesis 1; Acts 2). We each reflect the image of God. We have different strengths and capacities based on our natural abilities and temperaments—the way God made us—and we can adapt our *roles* to fit our *strengths*. Each individual is equally valuable and should be equally invested in the good of the cause, whether at work, at home, in church or in some other area of service. Each partner contributes his or her strengths and takes responsibility to work toward the well-being of the enterprise.

My friend Gini works as a legal assistant in one of those high-octane, take-no-prisoners litigation firms. Here's how different strengths/equal partners works for Gini and Ben (her husband) and Gini and Kevin (her boss).

> One of the things I really value is being part of a team. At home, it just makes things work better—Ben and I are able to evaluate who is the best "man" for the job. For instance, the church has implicitly taught for centuries that the man is head of the household finances. But I'm better at those things, making sure bills are paid on time, etc. So Ben delegates that to me, and I keep him in the loop. We struggled for years trying to have him do that stuff, and it was like a shoe that didn't fit.
>
> So we've made the whole roles thing more collaborative, deciding who is more suited to the task. I, being the big-picture gal, also am in charge of the calendar. When he kept his own calendar, we were always running into conflicting schedules. I really value being released into doing what I'm good at and appreciated for.
>
> In the workplace, that plays out like this: Kevin brings me into a case early on and tells me the big picture—what we are trying to accomplish, what issues are likely to come up, who the key players are and what I could do specifically to the case in terms of assistance. If there is someone unusually important or unusually temperamental involved, he lets me know that as well. That way, I always feel on top of things and less reactive.
>
> Kevin never treats me as "just" a secretary or hired fingers for typing purposes. Therefore, I am far less likely to say "it's not my job" and go on autopilot. Plus, that makes my job a whole lot more enjoyable, as I feel a real part of the deals rather than being sidelined. And I really care about it all, rather than thinking of it all as just a job and a paycheck. I feel invested.

Gini and Ben, and Gini and Kevin, have "different but equal" part-
nerships. Each person is important. Each contributes what he or
she does best. Each is invested in the good of the whole.

## Collaboration, Not Abdication

Christ delegated a position for husbands; you're the head of your
home (Ephesians 5:21-33). That means you're the one who's ultimately responsible for the *life* of your wife, marriage and family. So
use your position to serve (look out for, advance, support, create
the conditions that engender) their well-being. Think of "head" as
protection, making sure opportunities are not shut for your wife
and children, watching out to keep them safe from people and
systems that could damage them. Place yourself under Christ's authority and put their well-being first. I'm not suggesting that you
abdicate your responsibility, but consider soberly how you express
it. You can best fulfill your responsibility by honoring and collabo-
rating with your wife.

When Paul writes that wives must submit to their husbands, he
doesn't do it to give men a basis for being domineering to their
wives ("I'm the husband here. The Bible says you must submit to
me, woman!"). Domineering violates the spirit of the passage. In the
biblical view of marriage, husband and wife each take their cues
from Christ. Husbands *love* and wives *submit* in light of how Christ
loved and gave himself for the church.

Some husbands like to hold the "submit card" over their wife's
head. Some even like to use it, I'm sad to say, to keep their wives in
their "place." I rarely hear these same men talk about the stellar job
they do submitting themselves to the authorities—or to Jesus, for
that matter (1 Peter 2:13). Submitting starts with a recognition that
someone else is in a position of authority over us. That person has
the final say, makes the final decision. In the huddle on the football
field, the quarterback has the final say. On the sideline, it's the coach.

In the front office, it's the team's owner. In the White House Situation Room or with cabinet secretaries, the president wisely seeks counsel and input, but the final call—and weighty responsibility of the call—rests with the president. The president is the head.

Jesus is your head. Spend time paying attention to how you submit to him, and your wife might not have a problem submitting to you.

Just a thought.

## Guiding Principle #2

This one's especially for husbands: you and your wife are partners on the home front. Embrace that and be proactive about it. The home front is yours, together. It's not where you "help out" with the kids and run errands just to make her life go more smoothly. The home front is where you co-create, with Jesus, a foretaste of his kingdom. Your man-cave might be your sacred personal space, but home and family, present and future, the big picture and the details are yours too. You and her—Adam and Eve in the garden—cooking, cleaning, changing dirty diapers, getting up early with the little ones. Bring that mindset to your marriage and family.

You're an owner, not an add-on (not that she sees you that way, but your actions might make it look like you think that way). Owners take initiative. As Margaret, a young professional in the dental field, puts it:

> [I want him to] look for things that need to be done, as opposed to me asking. If you see laundry in a basket to be folded, fold it; if you know we're out of stuff from the grocery, swing by the store and pick it up; if the trash bins are full, empty them. I know that my husband, for example, has no problem actually *doing* whatever it is that needs to be done. However, if he volunteered to do them without my asking, I would not feel like I am nagging.

I also know my husband will offer: "Do you want me to stop by the grocery? Do you want me to fold the laundry?" I wish he would take initiative and do it, because if I have to answer the question, I feel insecure saying yes because I know he has had a long day at work. I don't want to say yes and seem like I'm *making* him stop to pick items up after work. I understand this is partnered with my needing to be more supportive if/when he does laundry and puts things in the wrong spot—not making a big deal out of it. Or if he buys the "wrong" kind of yogurt at the store. . . . If women, including me, continually discourage how men are doing things, no wonder there is no initiative.

## Working Together

What does it take to live out "different but equal"? To be present and engage fully? How does it look? Here's some of what I'm discovering, with the help of some of the women in my life.

First, in our heart of hearts, we have to value and embrace their dignity. We have to value them as those who bear the image with us. Kindra, a young female leader who works with refugees and others on the margins in the City Heights neighborhood of San Diego, has experienced more than her share of gender discrimination. She writes:

> There are many "things" that men could do [to work with and support the women leaders in their lives]—but the most important issue is the heart. If there is sexism or hatred in your heart, how will a law change that? If you just include women because you're forced to, then you aren't really including them at all. Men have made being a leader difficult by labeling strong women as bitchy. Don't call a woman a name because you would approach an issue or question differently. I've been called emotional, rebellious and guilty of practicing witch-

craft, all because I approached leadership differently from my male counterparts.

Kindra, who has a master's degree in theology and has almost completed her doctoral work, adds:

> I am created in God's very image, and I bring that holy perspective to the table. That ought to be honored, not feared or belittled. It's empowered me when I've been heard and, even if not fully understood, still given the freedom to try something my [female] way. Women can be a force for change without staging a coup. But this requires the voices that have been loudest and held longest to not just give the woman some room but maybe to take a vow of silence for a minute—to fully engage a different perspective and allow it light and ground to form healthy roots. I am not advocating a matriarchy to replace a patriarchy. I am supporting a shift in power [a sharing of power, a collaboration] that allows each person room to grow.

So, how do you feel about strong women (like Kindra)? About women who have the strength of "command" on StrengthsFinder or who are high Ds on the DiSC profile? Do you feel differently about men who are high Ds with the strength of command? If so, what's up with that?

Second, when we come to value and embrace their dignity, we can honor the differences between us. We can accept one another and what we each contribute to the whole. Lainie is more relational, I'm more task oriented. She's more verbal, I'm typically more inside my head. We know other couples who are just the opposite. Each strength is needed. Different is good.

Theresa works in student affairs at a university in North Texas and volunteers a ton of time in campus and church-related ministry with her husband. She writes of differences and strengths:

Utilize the natural strengths of each gender. I think men and women *both* should read a book, article, etc., to help each understand how the other thinks/communicates/acts so they can then see these differences as strengths instead of frustrations. Along these same lines, don't view emotions as a sign of weakness (in yourself or others). Rather, realize women have different strengths than men, and many times emotions/feelings stem from these strengths. So listen to what a woman is saying and understand where she's coming from. Then move forward with this new understanding. (I say this also knowing that sometimes emotions stem from wounds that haven't been attended to, in which case, listen with sympathy but do not allow unhealthy emotions to dictate your decisions.)

Holly Moore, vice president at Growing Leaders, would agree. She says:

Although some readers may disagree with me, no matter how accomplished I become as an executive, I will always be a female who processes information and makes decisions with a different mind-set than my male colleagues. The best male leaders in my career have been willing to embrace and accept my uniquely female perspective or reactions without showing disrespect for me as a business colleague or partner.[4]

Guys, what women add to the mix will enrich and advance the work of your team. Women often excel at candor, empathy, vulnerability and connectedness (not that some of you don't have these), traits shown to lead to greater success in the workplace, especially if you're trying to make your way in today's social economy. [5]

Three, watch out for insecurities. Are you secure enough to invite women to bring their strengths to the table? Secure enough to acknowledge that they might be stronger where you wish you were stronger? That they might have a trait that you wish you had? Theresa writes:

> I'd say both women and men need to be self-aware enough to recognize when they are allowing their own insecurities to affect their treatment of others. For example, a man might respond poorly to a woman in authority when he feels this threatens his perceived competence/ability to have the power/ability to provide. A woman might respond poorly to a man in authority if she reads everything through the grid of making sure she is treated properly as woman or if she assumes men are all women-haters, *or* if she has given into a culture that values men's general attributes more than women's.

Fourth, if you value and honor her dignity, support her in becoming who God made her to be and doing what God is calling her to do. Be supportive of her gifts and growth. Do that with the women you work with, whenever possible, but especially at home. My friend Linda is a trained marriage counselor and also works with her husband in their nonprofit. She says:

> Encourage men to look beyond their own goals and aspirations and to ask themselves, *Am I helping this woman to become all God wants her to be?* Husbands are privy to information as to what insecurities or wounds their wives have. They can ask God to show them how they can be an instrument for healing and growth in this particular woman. That may look different for each man and situation. They can either encourage or discourage, make it easy or difficult, lay on guilt or blessing. How?
>
> - Encourage and be supportive of her to further her education or training.
> - Put up some financial investment for her to start a business.

- Encourage her in a business or ministry opportunity.

- Take care of the kids even though it's inconvenient, so she can do something that's beneficial for her well-being.

This all means a lot of servant leadership from the husband and looking beyond what is best for him. And please remind men who have daughters that the way they treat and encourage their wives will greatly influence their daughters.

Fifth, go ballistic on violence against women, especially rape culture. While Christians fight each other over women serving in leadership roles in the church, the enemy's out devastating girls' and women's lives. Don't believe me? Consider female genital mutilation. And the kidnapping and selling of girls into the slave trade. And schoolgirls in Nigeria sold for twelve dollars as brides to militants. This cannot possibly be the world Jesus envisions for women. The God who created woman in God's image can't possibly be pleased with girls and women being oppressed and exploited in these ways. It's time for us to wake up to the war on women around the world—and across the hall. Kindra emailed me asking, *"Have you seen this?"* She was referring to a post about a New Zealand teen rape club.[6] She wrote:

Please pray for me. I see things like this . . . and well . . . ever since going to the round home in Manila, I am finding it hard to not freaking hate men. And I know—I mean, really I do—not all men are like this . . . but then there is this, and Steubenville,[7] and Soy Nana and Mark Driscoll and . . . *Ugh.* I am sick to death of it. Are you talking to the young men about this? How is your conversation changing things? Are you training differently than you were years ago, because this culture is sick and, man, we need some sober voices.

She added:

> Another hot topic, Daniel Tosh, who made a rape "joke" at a recent comedy show. He is one of the frat boys' heroes. One brave young woman spoke up and said she didn't think rape "jokes" were funny, to which Tosh replied, "Wouldn't it be funny if like five guys gang raped her right now?" The woman ran out in fear for her safety, as a room full of young men laughed.[8]

She felt outraged by these incidents, and rightly so. So do I. I'm a husband and a father of two daughters. If it had been my wife or one of my daughters who'd stood up to Tosh, only to be ridiculed by him, I can tell you from a place deep in my gut that it wouldn't have been funny at all. Not even close.

Not too long after she emailed me, I was gobsmacked by an article in *The Daily Campus* at Southern Methodist University, *my own backyard*, where the author felt the need to give college guys the "Top 10 Tips for Men to Avoid Committing Rape."[9] Let me be crystal clear: I'm glad the author spoke up, but I'm beyond dismayed that the article had to be written at all. Really, are you freaking kidding me? Has our culture come to this? Have we lost all sense of what it looks like to honor women? To protect them? To let a woman's no mean no? Have we become *that* infected by hookup culture and rape culture?

## Flipping Culture the Bird

What if we stood up and refused to accept culture's view of women? What if we worked with—and for—women instead of against them, over them or around them? What if we elevated the status of women out of a Genesis 1 view of their dignity and Acts 2 view of their place in the advancement of the purposes of God? What if we cared for them like Jesus did? What if, like Paul, we affirmed and celebrated women who work hard in the Lord? What if we woke up from our culture-induced slumber and stood up to the enemy's crippling of women (Luke 13:16)? What kind of world might we then create? Certainly a more life-giving world, a more Christ-honoring world.

What could you do to stand up for the dignity of women in the face of global oppression and exploitation? Here are a few suggestions:

- Boycott corporations and publications that oppress and objectify women (such as Hooters, Twin Peaks and Victoria's Secret, to name but a few of the more popular).

- Boycott humor, videos and cable channels that crack jokes about rape.

- Join an organization that advocates for women (check the list at womensorganizations.org).

- Read a book with your men's group that tells their story (like Leymah Gbowee's *Mighty Be Our Powers: How Sisterhood, Prayer, and Sex Changed a Nation at War*).

- Take a class that educates men on women's issues.

- Teach a class about women's issues to raise awareness.

- Start an organization to address the issues where they show up in your local area (like my friend Jerry Redman at Second Life Chattanooga).[10]

## Bringing It Home

It was a blustery spring day. I was nearing the end of a sixteen-mile training run for a marathon. I had my earphones in and had been listening to a combination of music and talks. I do long runs better when I can distract myself from the boredom of "one more mile." As I was running and listening, the words on the iPod faded into the background, and here's what I heard: "It's time to put preparation for Lainie's calling on the front burner of your lives."

We were living in Knoxville, Tennessee, and had been there about fifteen months. We had moved there to help some friends do work with emerging leaders. Our work with them was going well, and I had recently rented office space in a downtown high-rise and was getting traction for my coaching and consulting work with CEOs and their teams. Lainie and I weren't looking to move. But then I heard that statement: "It's time to put preparation for Lainie's calling on the front burner of your lives."

She felt drawn to serve as an ordained priest within the Anglican Communion. For that to happen, we knew she'd need a master of divinity degree (her discernment group had arrived at the same conclusion a couple of weeks earlier). So when I heard "It's time . . . ," I realized it might be time for her to do grad school, quite possibly moving from Knoxville. I shared what I had "heard" while running, encouraged her to pray and think about it, and suggested she start thinking about where she might want to study.

Through a series of events that quickly fell into place for us as well as conversations with friends and mentors, we discerned that the blustery-day thought was actually the next part of God's adventure for us. Four months later we moved to Dallas. Lainie had been accepted at Perkins School of Theology at Southern Methodist University (SMU). She enrolled in their MDiv program and would study for, as part of her degree, an Anglican Studies Certificate. The certificate was one reason Lainie selected Perkins. Another reason was their support for women in leadership roles in the church. Perhaps the strongest reason was that Elaine Heath, a strong female leader, innovator, professor and pastor, was at Perkins, and Lainie wanted to study under her.

I finished the first draft of this chapter while sitting in one of my favorite leather chairs at the Starbucks near the SMU campus. Lainie had just wrapped up her first semester at Perkins, with courses in Old Testament interpretation, the history of the

Christian movement, the church in its social context and New Testament Greek. She also met once a week in a spiritual formation group. In addition to her studies, she worked about eight hours a week as a chaplain to SMU undergrads.

For me, moving to Dallas to put preparation for her calling on the front burner meant making room for her, supporting her, encouraging her to live more fully into who she is and the work God has for her to do. I'm not a hero for doing that (in fact, she's done the same thing for me and my calling on more than one occasion), but I'm taking great joy in honoring her and watching her flourish.

- What do you think about the way Jesus treated women?

- If you were to work with the women in your life, what might it entail?

- If you were to stand up to end violence against women, where would you start?

### A Note from Lainie

It's Lainie here. I reentered grad school in August 2011, twenty-two years after my first master's degree. What a ride it's been—the best of times and some of the most demanding of times. The best because Daniel has championed me, cared for me, taken up the slack in the home for me, edited numerous papers for me. The best because of the opportunities for theological, emotional and spiritual development. Demanding because of how it has stretched me and challenged me to go beyond where I thought I could go.

Perkins has been a very safe place to wrestle with Scripture, God and others on pertinent life issues. Thinking about safe places to flourish brings me to this chapter of Daniel's book. I want to echo some of Daniel's thoughts briefly. These are *very real* struggles for most women I know:

- Having men "lord it over" or bully them in their home, church and workplace just because men can (or think they have permission to) power-up on them.

- Having men invalidate, disregard or feel threatened by women's concerns, ideas, talents, emotions—and the list goes on and on. Many times men don't follow women leaders well, and this is not good for the morale of the workplace or anyplace in society.

- Husbands using "I'm the head of this home" as a trump card any time they want something to happen—or not to happen. It's *way* overused, guys. Please stop! If it's never used again until the end of temporal time, it will not balance all the times it has been used to mistreat and abuse women.

- Having husbands pat themselves on the back because they're such great helpers at home. Really? What kinds of accolades would you get at work if, as a codirector, all you did was say, "Tell me what to do. I'm here to help," assuming your codirector has to tell you what to do?

# PART FOUR

# SUPPORTED

## Connecting with Those Who Help Us

*Follow me
and **I** will make you
fishers of men.*

**Jesus**

*Maybe we can all do together
what we could not do separately.*

**Bill D., AA's Member 3**

**15**

# MENTORS

## Seek and Share Wisdom

*But when he, the Spirit of truth, comes,*
*he will guide you into all the truth.*

**Jesus in John 16:13**

*And the things you have heard me say*
*in the presence of many witnesses*
*entrust to reliable people who will*
*also be qualified to teach others.*

**2 Timothy 2:2**

Let me introduce you to some significant people in my life, people
God has sent my way to help me answer the summons to live and
lead with Jesus. French Arrington taught me New Testament
Greek. Don Bowdle taught me the book of Hebrews and the
Gospel of John. Dawn Waring taught me Old Testament Hebrew.

Bobby Clinton taught me how God shapes leaders. Jim Kouzes and Barry Posner taught me how to address my leadership challenges.

Jeremy Stefano and Buddy Odom helped me pay attention to the Spirit's "directing of my life." Donald Weaver taught me how to cultivate mindsight. Saint Ignatius helped me understand that God is "Love loving." Dan Reeves trained me to facilitate mentoring groups with midcareer leaders. Tom Paterson trained me to lead cross-functional strategic-planning sessions.

Susan Regas helped me unpack emotional and family-of-origin baggage. Lana Whisman guided me through a second round of emotional healing. Van Shubin worked with me on a third round.

Don Price invited me to work at The Valley Cathedral. Terry Walling sponsored me into Church Resource Ministries. Reilly Flynn paved the way for me to work with a group of his friends at the University of Virginia.

What have I just listed?

Different types of mentors I've had: teachers, spiritual directors, trainers, counselors and sponsors. Most were older than I, some younger. A few of my mentors were historical; most were contemporary. Several worked with me over long periods. Each passed along resources I needed in my development as a person or as a leader. Without them or others like them, I wouldn't be where I am today. Some mentored me personally in life-on-life relationships, others through their writings.

I want to take a look at mentoring in this chapter. Why? First, because your life will be richer, fuller, broader and deeper through what mentors pass on to you. Second, to encourage you to return the favor by mentoring others who need the resources you can share. Third, because you won't get where you need to go without mentors.

Mentors can keep you in the game, help you avoid plateauing in your development and keep you listening to God and maintaining a learning posture. In short, they connect you with God-given resources that empower your personal and professional development. Over the course of our lives, we'll need several mentors and mentors of different types. They'll come from inside and outside our organizations. Some will be peer, some will be our "juniors," and some will be above us on the organizational chart or in age and life experience.

## Definition

What is mentoring? "Mentoring is a relational experience in which one person empowers another by sharing God-given resources."[1] Let's break it down.

Mentoring is a relational experience. That means it happens best when there's a personal *connection* between the mentor and the mentoree. (Sometimes this is impossible, as in the case of the historical mentor.) The relationship could be short-term or long-term, formal or informal, planned or spontaneous, depending on the type of mentor and the design of the mentoring relationship.

The key part of the relationship is the *attraction* between the mentor and mentoree. Each sees in the other a reason to connect and pass along (the mentor) or receive (the mentoree) some type of resource. The resource could include access to an organization, a group or a certain leader; a new way to solve a problem; a new skill for accomplishing a certain task; wisdom gained through life experience; knowledge about a particular subject; or whatever else the mentor can provide that the mentoree needs. The mentor shares resources with the mentoree, and the mentoree is thereby empowered to do (or know or be or feel) what could not be done (at least to the same extent) prior to the exchange.

Who's been a significant mentor to you thus far? What kind of relationship did you share with that person? What resource did the mentor pass along? In what way were you empowered to grow as a result of the mentoring relationship?

Here's an example of a short-term mentoring exchange between Moses and his father-in-law, Jethro:

> The next day Moses took his seat to serve as judge for the people, and they stood around him from morning till evening. When his father-in-law saw all that Moses was doing for the people, he said, "What is this you are doing for the people? Why do you alone sit as judge, while all these people stand around you from morning till evening?"
>
> Moses answered him, "Because the people come to me to seek God's will. Whenever they have a dispute, it is brought to me, and I decide between the parties and inform them of God's decrees and instructions."
>
> Moses' father-in-law replied, "What you are doing is not good. You and these people who come to you will only wear yourselves out. The work is too heavy for you; you cannot handle it alone. Listen now to me and I will give you some advice, and may God be with you. You must be the people's representative before God and bring their disputes to him. Teach them his decrees and instructions, and show them the way they are to live and how they are to behave. But select capable men from all the people—men who fear God, trustworthy men who hate dishonest gain—and appoint them as officials over thousands, hundreds, fifties and tens. Have them serve as judges for the people at all times, but have them bring every difficult case to you; the simple cases they can decide themselves. That will make your load lighter, because they will share it with you. If you do this and God so commands, you will be able to stand the strain, and all these people will go home satisfied." (Exodus 18:13-23)

What do we have here? Moses the judge of the people, doing his work—resolving conflicts and settling disputes. That's good, right? The *work* is, but not the *way* Moses is doing the work.

Jethro (the mentor) identifies a problem. He sees that Moses (the mentoree) will exhaust himself and frustrate the people by continuing to do the work the way he's doing it. Jethro knows a better way and shares it with Moses. Moses takes him up on the better way and is thereby empowered to do the work more effectively. That's how mentoring works. It's not always as compressed as this example, but it can be.

Other examples from the Bible? Bezalel and Oholiab taught their fellow craftsmen the knowledge and skills needed for carving wood, setting gemstones and working with metals and fabrics (Exodus 35:30-35). Barnabas sponsored Paul into the church at Antioch (Acts 11:25-26). Priscilla and Aquila taught Apollos "the way of God more adequately" (Acts 18:24-26). Paul taught Timothy the qualifications for elders in the church at Ephesus (1 Timothy 3:1-12). As a result of these mentoring exchanges, furnishings for the tabernacle were designed and created. New converts were established in their faith. Apollos was empowered to preach a fuller message about God's work in and through Jesus. Timothy was prepared to identify, select and appoint elders.

## Misconceptions

As you seek out a mentor—and decide to mentor others—don't let these common mentoring misconceptions trip you up.

***Mentors have to be older than mentorees.*** Wrong. Several of my mentors have been younger than me. The heart of the mentoring relationship is not age, but *empowerment* gained through the resources your mentor will share with you. Again, the resources can include life experiences, new perspectives, wisdom, a set of skills, a timely book to read, a certain way to solve a problem, how coffee is roasted and beer brewed, or others. Age is sometimes a factor, but not always.

*You can have only one mentor.* We sometimes think of Moses mentoring Joshua, of Jesus mentoring the apostles and of Paul mentoring Timothy, and from that we conclude we can have only one mentor. Actually Scripture doesn't name all the people who mentored these leaders. It names at least one who had a primary influence on each of their lives, sure, but it doesn't intend to say they had only one mentor. Take a look at my list at the beginning of the chapter. I identified eighteen people who've mentored me. I could name another five to ten who've played a significant role in my life.

Some of my mentors have worked with me longer than others, some have worked with me on items of special significance, and some have been more formal and intentional in their relationships with me. But each mentor on the list has empowered me by sharing resources with me.

*Your one special mentor can get you everything you need for every area of your life.* False. No one is that knowledgeable or skillful. You can actually have several different types of mentors: disciplers, spiritual directors, trainers, counselors, teachers, sponsors, contemporary models and historical models.

*I don't know enough to mentor anyone else.* Actually, what God has given you, you can share with others who need it. "Anyone can mentor," say Clinton and Stanley, "provided he has learned something from God and is willing to share with others what he has learned."[2]

## Who Do You Need?

Below are seven types of mentors, with a brief description of the empowerment that each type provides. If you need a mentor at this point in your life, you might need one of these types. If someone is seeking you out for a mentoring relationship, he or she probably sees in you something related to one of these types.

*1. Discipler.* A discipler helps you develop sound knowledge and habits in the fundamentals of knowing and following Jesus. Philip did this with the Ethiopian eunuch (Acts 8:26-40), and Paul performed a similar role alongside Barnabas, in his first year with the Christians at Antioch (Acts 11:22-30). If you need to grow in the fundamentals of the Christian faith, you might need a discipler.

**2. *Spiritual director.*** A spiritual director helps you learn to pay attention to how the Spirit is directing you. Two of my mentors, Jeremy Stefano and Buddy Odom, are trained spiritual directors. They helped me develop my capacity to be attentive and responsive to the Spirit and the ways in which the Spirit speaks. A spiritual director's work is crucial because so many of us come to periods when God grows silent (it seems). Or God starts communicating with us in ways that aren't familiar to us. We hit the wall. We get stuck. We lose our way. Spiritual directors can help us tune in to how God is speaking, see the work God is doing and come to terms with where we find ourselves. If you're finding it difficult to perceive what God is doing in your life or to see how the Spirit is guiding you, or if you just want to become more sensitive to the Spirit, you might need a spiritual director.

**3. *Trainer.*** Clinton and Stanley describe this type as a coach, but I use the term *trainer* to distinguish it from how the International Coaching Federation defines the work of a coach. A trainer imparts motivation, knowledge and skills needed to perform a certain role or function. Jethro served Moses as a trainer when he introduced him to a new framework for resolving disputes among the people and motivated him to use the new way. Bezalel and Oholiab trained their fellow artisans for creating the tabernacle furnishings. If you need to learn new skills, you probably need a trainer.

**4. *Counselor.*** The counselor asks insightful questions, provides timely insights and introduces conceptual frameworks for understanding emotional and relational issues. I wrote about one of my counselors, Susan Regas, in the chapter on baggage. If you feel stuck in your relationships, you might need a counselor.

**5. Teacher.** A teacher imparts information about a particular topic; he has knowledge of a certain subject. Teachers are one of the most common types of mentors most people have had. If you need to learn new concepts or deepen your understanding of a particular subject, you would probably benefit from a teacher.

**6. Sponsor.** A sponsor opens doors for you and gives you access to other leaders or organizations. I referred earlier to Don Price and Terry Walling. Each of these men gave me access to an organization—the one they worked with. I ended up serving with their organizations because of their mentor-sponsor role in my life. When people sponsor you, they're lending you their credibility; they're putting their reputation on the line for you. They're opening doors. If you need help gaining access to a group or to certain individuals, you might need a sponsor.

**7. Models.** Either through their lives or work, models set an example that others aspire to learn from or imitate. The contemporary model provides a current living example. The historical model inspires us from a previous time period. I've worked with young men who've been inspired by Seth Godin, Steve Jobs, Bono, John F. Kennedy, C. S. Lewis, Augustine, Luther, Calvin and St. Anthony of the Desert. These are famous people, no doubt, but contemporary and historical models don't have to be famous nor do they have to be men. However, they do have to set an example, either in their personal lives or professions, that inspires and informs how you want to live or work or lead. I imagine you can list those who serve as contemporary or historical models for you. I hope you'll also live in a way that inspires others to want to emulate your example.

## Maximizing Mentoring

When you see that you need a mentor or when you think of someone you'd like to reach out to as a mentor, keep the fol-

lowing dynamics in mind: attraction, responsiveness, accountability, definition and debriefing.

**Attraction.** This fuels the relationship. Without it, you won't feel
drawn to connect. Attraction happens because the mentor and
mentoree sense that empowerment can take place, that there's
something to be gained through the relationship. See if you can
hear the attraction in the following email.

Dear David,

I hope that everything is going well. I am emailing you to see
if you would be interested in being a spiritual mentor for me.
Over the past, I have sought older male figures who can guide
me through life (e.g. marriage, spirituality, and a Christlike
attitude). After being at your place the other week, I felt that
I can make an honest connection with you. Please let me
know what you think or if you have the time to pursue this.

Peace,

Frank

Frank had been to David's house for dinner, and David had
shared some stories from his grad school days. The stories, and
David's demeanor, led Frank to feel he could connect with him at a
heart level. That's the attraction factor. It means that the mentor
and mentoree see something in each other that enables the formation of the mentoring relationship. David sensed a teachable and
humble spirit in Frank, so he agreed to have a couple of conversations with him to explore what type of mentoring relationship
might work. *Attraction* makes mentoring possible.

**Responsiveness.** This is what keeps the relationship moving
forward. The mentoree must respond positively to input from the
mentor. This requires a teachable spirit—a responsive attitude—
from the mentoree and an attentive posture from the mentor.

*Accountability.* If you're setting up a formal mentoring relationship with regular meetings and interactions, make sure you put accountability mechanisms in place. Your mentor will want to know how best to hold you accountable. And you'll want to hold your mentor accountable to do what he—or she—promised. Accountability ensures commitment.

*Definition.* You need to define the relationship. Start by defining the purpose. What are you hoping to gain from the relationship? In the example above, Frank mentioned that he was looking for a spiritual mentor, someone who could "guide me through life." For the relationship to work well, he and David would need to clarify the purpose. Without definition, David wouldn't know whether he could help Frank.

Once you have the purpose defined, decide how to achieve it. Each type of mentoring relationship has its own set of expectations. Teachers will probably have reading assignments for you to complete. Trainers will likely want you to practice certain skills. Disciplers might want you to memorize Scriptures. Clarify who will do what, by when.

Then plan your calendar. How long will the mentoring relationship last? How often will you meet? When and where will you meet? Schedule one or two times (perhaps monthly) to evaluate the mentoring relationship. Talk about how it's going, whether expectations are being met and whether modifications need to be made.

At the end, review the full experience. Celebrate the progress made. Bring it to a close. If you want to continue, discuss that as well.

*Debriefing.* When you actually meet for mentoring sessions or conversations, debrief. A good debrief, based on a discipleship tool used by InterVarsity Christian Fellowship, follows a cycle of reviewing, learning and application.[3]

InterVarsity has found that debriefing deepens formation. Here are sample questions that can be used:

1. Review (in light of previous action steps or assignments)

What happened?

What was the experience like for you?

Where did you feel stuck, afraid, affirmed or excited?

Where did you experience God?

2. Learn (identify lessons)

What are you learning? About yourself? Others? God?

What did you expect from this experience and what surprised you?

What might God be teaching you from the experience?

3. Apply (prepare for application)

In light of what you learned, how will things be different in the future?

What is your next step?

What is the one thing God might be inviting you to do next?

What might you need to improve, change or keep doing?

Who is one person you can share this with?

If you design your mentoring relationship with these dynamics in mind—attraction, responsiveness, accountability, definition and debriefing—you'll be much more likely to benefit from it. If you leave out one of them, or take an attitude of "let's just show up and see what will happen," you'll be less likely to experience the empowerment that mentoring can provide.

God will bring mentors into your life. Those mentors can help you stay in the game and help you continue living and leading with Jesus. When you mentor others, you can do the same for them.

• Which type of mentor might you need right now?

• Who do you know that could fill that role?

• What could you do to reach out to that person?

• Who might need you to be his or her mentor?

## 16

# OTHER MEN

## Connect with Spiritual Fathers
## and Brothers

*When they landed, they saw a fire of burning coals there*
*with fish on it, and some bread. . . . Jesus said to them,*
*"Come and have breakfast."*

**John 21:9, 12**

Eight men sat around the fire pit. This was the first time they'd all been together. Six of them had taken part in a training workshop the three previous days. They were still getting acquainted. Two had just arrived and were being introduced. Warmed by the fire that crisp autumn evening, they shared life stories, savored the steak and fish dinner they'd just enjoyed and looked forward to libations that would soon be served.

Eight men. Six were "fathers"—men of depth and experience with life, marriage, work and seeking after Jesus. They'd been together in a workshop the three previous days. Two were "sons"— young men in their twenties who were wrapping up their first quarter of life, men with their own experiences and stories to tell. They were good friends, "brothers," who'd been through some thick and thin together, who had learned to open their hearts to one another. They loved Jesus and sought to follow him, but had grown up in different church expressions of that.

One of the fathers, who knew the two sons, had invited them to the impromptu fire-pit gathering. He wanted them to sit by the fire and meet some veterans of life's ups and downs, men with battle scars who walked with a limp—and with the aroma of Jesus. These fathers cared about sons.

Drinks were poured. Stogies lit. More logs tossed on the fire. More jokes and laughter all around. Predictions about the weekend's football games. Good-natured banter. Then one of the fathers, the host of the gathering, who'd invited the two sons, rolled a grenade into the middle of the group—rolled it right by the hissing, popping flames. Not a real one, but a live one nonetheless. It was a question about the nature and work of the Holy Spirit.

He knew the sons had been wrestling with the question. He wanted them to see how their newfound friends would come at it. He wanted to provoke some deeper questions, stir up a different flame, get the sparks flying.

An hour later, after the fathers had offered their collective perspectives and after further dialogue and interaction with the son-brothers, one of the fathers leaned in, looked at the sons and asked, "Are we gonna talk this thing to death, or shall we pray? Sounds like there's something maybe you two are looking for? Maybe it's something you want to ask Jesus about?"

One of the sons was holding back. He didn't know the older men around the fire, so he wasn't sure he could trust them. That was understandable, but his brother called him out. His brother knew he was holding back—maybe even hiding a little. His brother knew what he needed to take to Jesus, and he named it.

Turned out, both of them had something they wanted to take to Jesus. So the fathers went with them to Jesus in prayer. And Jesus met them. He gave both those sons something they needed that night. And he gave the fathers something they needed too.

As the patio fire quietly died out, other fires flamed up. For one of the sons, it was a fire of forgiveness for his father. For the other son, it was a fire of confidence for a next step at work. For the father who'd rolled out the grenade, it was a fire of affirmation—of seeing what could happen for young men in his city.

Amazing things can happen when fathers and sons, brothers young and old, meet around a fire pit in the presence of Jesus, when they meet—not to control each other, not to manipulate each other, not to mandate a certain decision be made, not to force one another into a certain mold—but to go to Jesus together.

When I say amazing things can happen, I mean that *life* can break in, the King can bring his kingdom in whatever way *the King* sees fit: sins convicted, sins forgiven, health restored, confidence bolstered, direction clarified, relationships mended, vision imparted, gifts of the Spirit released and bestowed, hope renewed, hearts broken, pride uncovered, character deepened, questions settled, love unleashed. And Jesus honored.

Life can overcome death around the fire pit, in the presence of Jesus.

I was there, one of the six fathers who helped take the sons to Jesus. I was part of their blessing that night, the breaking out of *life*, and they were part of the blessing I received. Jesus brought eight men together, and through their gathering, helped each one continue living and leading with him. Jesus does that. He brings brothers, spiritual fathers and sons into our lives to help us keep walking and working with him, strengthening each other for the journey.

## Charcoal Fire

As I reflect on that October evening, another fire pit comes to mind. Seven men are together—brothers, mostly—and a wise one, a father, shows up. He starts a charcoal fire, waits, cooks up some breakfast, and invites the men to come and eat. John tells us the story of Jesus making this post-resurrection appearance to seven of his apostles who've gone fishing:

> Afterward Jesus appeared again to his disciples, by the Sea of Galilee. It happened this way: Simon Peter, Thomas (also known as Didymus), Nathanael from Cana in Galilee, the sons of Zebedee, and two other disciples were together. "I'm going out to fish," Simon Peter told them, and they said, "We'll go with you." So they went out and got into the boat, but that night they caught nothing.
>
> Early in the morning, Jesus stood on the shore, but the disciples did not realize that it was Jesus. He called out to them, "Friends, haven't you any fish?" "No," they answered. He said, "Throw your net on the right side of the boat and you will find some." When they did, they were unable to haul the net in because of the large number of fish.
>
> Then the disciple whom Jesus loved said to Peter, "It is the Lord!" As soon as Simon Peter heard him say, "It is the Lord," he wrapped his outer garment around him (for he had taken it off) and jumped into the water. The other disciples followed in the boat, towing the net full of fish, for they were not far from shore, about a hundred yards. When they landed, they saw a fire of burning coals there with fish on it, and some bread.
>
> Jesus said to them, "Bring some of the fish you have just caught." So Simon Peter climbed back into the boat and dragged the net ashore. It was full of large fish, 153, but even with so many the net was not torn. Jesus said to them, "Come

and have breakfast." None of the disciples dared ask him, "Who are you?" They knew it was the Lord. Jesus came, took the bread and gave it to them, and did the same with the fish. This was now the third time Jesus appeared to his disciples after he was raised from the dead.

When they had finished eating, Jesus said to Simon Peter, "Simon son of John, do you love me more than these?"

"Yes, Lord," he said, "you know that I love you."

Jesus said, "Feed my lambs."

Again Jesus said, "Simon son of John, do you love me?"

He answered, "Yes, Lord, you know that I love you."

Jesus said, "Take care of my sheep."

The third time he said to him, "Simon son of John, do you love me?"

Peter was hurt because Jesus asked him the third time, "Do you love me?" He said, "Lord, you know all things; you know that I love you."

Jesus said, "Feed my sheep. Very truly I tell you, when you were younger you dressed yourself and went where you wanted; but when you are old you will stretch out your hands, and someone else will dress you and lead you where you do not want to go." Jesus said this to indicate the kind of death by which Peter would glorify God. Then he said to him, "Follow me!"

Peter turned and saw that the disciple whom Jesus loved was following them. (This was the one who had leaned back against Jesus at the supper and had said, "Lord, who is going to betray you?") When Peter saw him, he asked, "Lord, what about him?" (John 21:1-21)

This story points the way for men who want to make it a regular practice to meet together around the fire pit. So I want to look at what these verses tell us about Jesus and what that can mean for our fire-pit groups.[1] Then I'll say who I think we need around the fire pit with us and conclude the chapter by suggesting some principles for setting up and facilitating such groups.

## Jesus and Our Fire-Pit Groups

John's primary focus in chapter 21 of his Gospel is Jesus. Peter and John are in the story and are important to the story, but Jesus is the focus. And what John tells us about Jesus is crucial for our fire-pit groups.

*Jesus is Lord.* Throughout his Gospel, John has declared the deity of Jesus. Here he uses the fishing story to drive home the point that Jesus is God's Son. Jesus knows where the fish are, and after their futile night of fishing, he tells the seven men exactly where to find them. Further, this is a post-resurrection appearance, and Jesus is Lord over both nature and death. Jesus is Lord over all.

What does it mean for our fire-pit groups that Jesus is Lord? It means that Jesus sees all and knows all. He knows what's best for each person around the fire pit, so we should entrust each other to Jesus. As Lord, only Jesus can call the shots for each person in our groups. I can't and you can't. The men in our groups don't have to do what we say. They can choose to go their own way. We're there to serve and encourage them, and to create an environment where they can connect with Jesus. We're not there to control, coerce or manipulate. Jesus is Lord. We should entrust each other to his wisdom and care. The men in our groups answer to Jesus, not to us.

*Jesus is host and server.* He takes the initiative and convenes this meeting. It's his idea. He prepares the breakfast and serves it. The breakfast meal recalls previous scenes from John's Gospel where Jesus hosted or served, like the wine-making miracle at the wedding in Cana, the miracle of feeding the five thousand on the Galilean hillside and the Last Supper. Jesus is host and server.

What does this mean for our fire-pit groups? That we should take our cues for each meeting from him. The reason we have men meeting around fire pits in the first place is that Jesus wants it. He gives the idea for the group to form. He convenes the meeting. So we can trust him to serve whatever soul food or drink is needed at each meeting. One night he might serve prime rib. Another night he might serve peanut butter and jelly sandwiches. Either way, it's up to him. He's the host and server.

If you're leading a group, you're the second in command. You serve at Jesus' pleasure. Look to him. Take your cues from him. Seek him for how to arrange a particular meeting and for how to make adjustments once the meeting is underway.

***Jesus gives his followers what they need now.*** After the breakfast, Jesus takes Peter on a stroll along the seashore and initiates a conversation. They have some unfinished business to discuss. Jesus wants to hear what Peter loves most. He wants to see how Peter has been affected by his three-time denial on the night that Jesus was betrayed. He wants to talk about what could easily be left unsaid between them.

Why? What's the point of this exchange? Jesus is Lord, right? He sees all and knows all. He already knows the answers to the questions he's asking Peter. He already knows Peter's heart. So what's Jesus doing?

He's restoring Peter. Jesus steps in, calls Peter aside and gives him what he needs most: restoration. Jesus gives his followers what they need now—and what they need most.

What does this mean for our fire-pit groups? That we shouldn't force meetings into a certain mold. A typical format is good, a liturgy even, but let each meeting ebb and flow as Jesus leads. Let him direct attention to a particular theme or person on any given night.

Read the narrative of John 21 again. Notice what Jesus gives Peter: three opportunities to say out loud that he loves Jesus; three statements of commissioning to lead the new community; a glimpse into Peter's future; a reminder that John was Jesus' concern not

Peter's; and a sharp command: "Follow me." In 115 words (in English) Jesus restored, commissioned, inspired, challenged, tenderized and strengthened Peter.

Can you accomplish that in a fire-pit meeting? Of course not. Neither can I.

You can't possibly design a meeting that will do what Jesus can do. But you don't have to. You don't have to bear the burden of taking care of everybody's needs. Jesus will do that. Jesus alone *can* do that. And Jesus alone should do that. You and me, our motives are too mixed. Our wounds still hold way too much sway in our lives. Sure, we can encourage our brothers and fathers. Sure, we can suggest to them that perhaps we have a thought to share with them that might be helpful, given what we know they're going through. But only Jesus can shine the light into dark places and bring healing to the hurt places. Only Jesus can say what they actually need to hear *now*.

Invite Jesus to speak. Then get out of his way.

*Jesus appoints his followers to their place in his story.* During their conversation, Jesus starts talking with Peter about tending and shepherding a flock. This is the language of commissioning. Jesus is appointing Peter to a leadership role in the community. The language is reminiscent of Psalm 78:70-72, where the writer tells us that the Lord took David from tending his father's sheep and made him shepherd (king/leader) over his people, Israel. Here on the seashore, after the bread-and-fish breakfast over the charcoal fire, Jesus appoints Peter to a shepherding leadership role in the new community. (Yes, Peter had already been designated as an apostle. This is a specific post-denial commission to shepherd.)

What does this mean for our fire-pit groups? Jesus appoints his followers to their place in the story. But don't rush ahead of him when you think you might know what their place is. Jesus walked and worked with Peter for *three years* prior to this conversation.

When I'm with a group of men, I have to hold myself back on this one. I want people to know their specific calling, especially young men who are chomping at the bit to get in the game. I want to lay it out for them in flashing neon lights. But that's not my place. Sure, I can spot what they have energy for. I can see, over time, what they really care about. I can even identify what they're good at, if we have enough time together. *But I can't appoint them to their place in the story, because it's not my story.* I'm neither the hero nor the author. Jesus is.

So I have to hold back. Wait on Jesus. Point them to Jesus. And I have to do that when we're meeting together around the fire pit, when the flames are burning hot and I think I know what they need to do with their lives. I also have to do it when we're away from the fire pit and its embers have grown cold.

## Participants

Who do you want around the fire pit with you? I want *men who will commit to following Jesus together.* When I say "men," I mean other males who know what it's like to be a male and to deal with male issues. I mean different ages and worldviews: fathers, sons and brothers. Each brings a unique gift to the mix. Fathers bring depth, maturity, experience and wisdom that sons lack. Sons add fresh energy, new ideas and zeal. They keep fathers fresh, youthful and aware of the future.

Brothers bring a close-in-age commonality of perspective, strength and playfulness. They see through your bravado. They know your crap. Maybe you think they don't, but they do. They know when you're posturing and bluffing. And they'll fight with you, or razz you, as the situation warrants.

By "commit" I mean make it a priority to be with each other consistently. To show up and contribute to group gatherings. To be together informally outside of group meetings. To help each other do life.

When I say "together," I mean trusting, honest, open friendships of love and support. Around your fire pit will be friends who know your issues, call you out and love you. That means you'll need to be transparent and vulnerable. I read somewhere that transparency is letting others see you. Vulnerability is asking for and receiving their help and care—and their loving correction, if needed.

Yeah, I know. A lot of us guys hate the weakness and vulnerability stuff. We believe the lie that we're the only one who is weak, the only one who struggles. So we try to hide it, and our capacity for creating true friendships stays locked up inside us. The sooner we get past the myth of the all-powerful male, the sooner we can get healed and get on with living more freely and wholeheartedly.

One of my mentors told me that we're as sick as the secrets we keep and the sins we hide. She was right. Bring it into the light. Ask your brothers to take you to Jesus. Tell them to make like you're the paralytic in Mark 2:1-12 and to haul you into God's presence, digging through or knocking down any obstacles or structures that get in the way. Swallow your pride, admit your struggle, and ask for help.

Who needs to be around the fire pit? Men who will commit to follow Jesus together. Fathers, sons and brothers who will stand side by side, heart to heart, and walk through life with Jesus and one another.

### Fire-Pit Principles

My brothers and sons in Knoxville taught me how to build a fire, literally and figuratively. They used the log cabin method, stacking the logs in a square shape, with room between for airflow and kindling in the middle. Once the fire began to flame up, they'd lay other logs on top like they were building a roof. This made for a hot fire that burned well throughout the night.

They were gracious to me as we discovered some guidelines for fire-pit meetings. For the first few cycles of meetings, we didn't know we were creating a new way of being together. They couldn't have known, because I didn't know either. I didn't realize what was happening until we were about sixteen weeks into meeting together. I've combined some of what I learned with them, what I learned with the men in my Charlottesville group and what I learned about leading mentoring groups with midcareer and emerging leaders in the principles below.

***Establish a clear purpose together, then do your purpose.*** Don't waver from it unless you renegotiate with the men around the fire pit. In Charlottesville and Knoxville, we said it this way: "We meet together to encourage one another as men following Jesus. Because each word matters, men—following—Jesus, we'll give attention to each word during various group meetings." For example, we spent our first six gatherings in Knoxville just looking at stories of Jesus in the Bible.

If some men don't want to meet to commit to your purpose, that's fine. Could be they're not ready. Could be your gathering isn't the right one for them. Don't let that deter you, and don't lay any guilt on them.

***Adopt a standard format.*** This will free you from being dependent on any one leader's personality. The power will be in the group process, not in a particular leader's giftedness.

In Charlottesville, we took the first hour for dinner and updates on the previous week. Each person had a few minutes to talk about what was going well and what wasn't, what he was thankful for and asking for, or other such conversation starters that moved us from surface level to heart level. We took the second hour to read and reflect on Scripture, then to pray together.

In Knoxville, in the first part of our meetings, we would quiet ourselves in silence. Then we'd play a song or read a Scripture to prompt conversation with Jesus, out loud, around the group. We'd do next whatever seemed appropriate: a second round of sharing;

prayer for one or two people who especially needed it that night; some type of experiential learning; or just sitting a bit longer with Jesus. This lasted from forty-five to ninety minutes, depending on the evening. Then we'd move to a more relaxed time of informal banter, food, drinks, laughter and catching up. The guys were free to leave after the first part. Most would stay around for the second.

*State your purpose every week.* Say what you are. Say what you are not. Here's what we said in Knoxville:

- We're a group of men who want to encourage one another to follow Jesus in every area of our lives.

- We're not a Bible study, but we often read and reflect on Scripture.

- We're not a "small group." We're a group of men who meet together to encourage one another and talk out loud to Jesus.

- We're not accountability partners, but we do want to be brothers and allies.

- We're not an intercession group, but we do talk to Jesus together.

- We're not a support group, and we're not here to fix one another, but we will pray for you. Ask for help, and we'll share what we can. We won't force anything on you.[2]

- We're not a worship group, but we sometimes sing to Jesus.

- We're not trying to build community. We're not even sure what that word means. But we do want to build heart-to-heart friendships and learn to care for one another.

- We emphasized repeatedly that we gathered to focus, first, on time with Jesus, in the company of one another. That first, we would speak with Jesus. We could speak with one another later.

*Set clear guidelines.* How often will you meet? Where? What will the start time and stop time be? Are there any other rules of the game that you'll follow? We had guidelines like these:

- When talking to Jesus, use a few short sentences. Don't preach to the group or monopolize the time. Since some of us are more talkative than others, be sure to make room for everyone to speak.

- You don't have to talk if you don't want to.

- Turn off or silence cell phones. This time is set apart to be with Jesus and one another. Tell your wife or girlfriend that your phone will be off.

- What we say or pray stays in the group, unless we're given permission to share it with others. That includes wives and girlfriends.

- We're not here to hype anything. If Jesus has peanut butter and jelly for us, fine. If he has a display of Spirit-power, fine. The point is *Jesus*—being with Jesus, in the company of one another.

- We start on time and end on time. If the host invites us to stay later, fine. If not, convene elsewhere for round two, if you want to.

***Set up on-ramps and off-ramps.*** Provide opportunities for men to leave or join. Life situations change, so honor that. Others might want to join, so create opportunities where that's appropriate. Decide how many weeks you'll meet in any particular cycle of meetings (six weeks? twelve? sixteen?). When I started the Knoxville group, I said to the guys: "We're going to try this for six weeks and see what happens. If we want to keep going, fine. If not, fine. This might not be the right group for you, and that's okay. This isn't a litmus test for friendship."

These guidelines, and others like them, established helpful boundaries for our fire-pit gatherings in Charlottesville and Knoxville. Along with our focus on Jesus and the encouragement we tried to be for one another, they made our gatherings more life-giving for the fathers, son and brothers who met together.

God not only summons us, shapes us and sends us, God also sends men with whom we can share our lives. Men with whom we can meet with Jesus. Men who'll make our lives richer and fuller. Men who'll help us answer the summons to live and lead with Jesus.

• Who are those men in your life?

• What are you doing to connect with them?

• What could you do to strengthen those connections?

# CONCLUSION

*Follow me,*
*and I will make you*
*fishers of men.*

**Jesus**

*At once they left their nets*
*and followed him.*

**Matthew 4:20**

Everybody has a story. Andrew and Peter, James and John left their nets and family businesses to accept the summons to live and lead with Jesus. Because they did, because they followed Jesus, we can know their stories, and their stories can touch our lives (as they have touched the lives of millions through the centuries).

Part of your story has been written and can now be told, *but other parts of your story have yet to be written.* Those parts will be written based on choices you make now and in the days ahead.

Your story will show that you've been summoned and shaped to

live and lead with Jesus for the life of the world, but what will it
show after that? Where do you go from here? What's your next
step? You don't have to have the future sorted out, but what's your
next step?

Kyle is heading out to serve on the PTA of his son's elementary
school. He wants to create a more life-giving culture for students
and teachers. Gordon is heading to grad school to study theology
and earn a teaching certificate. He wants to prepare himself to
teach theology to high school students; he wants to pass on God's
story to them. John is suiting up in surgical greens and heading into
a hospital delivery room so he can hold his wife's hand as she de-
livers their first child by C-section. He wants to be present to
welcome his son into the world.

Spencer is starting a brew club for his neighborhood. He wants
to have men over, build friendships and ask the Holy Spirit for opportunities to share God's love. Greg has accepted a new assignment
at work. He's forgoing many of the perks usually associated with his
position so he can model a new teamwork-based culture. Clint is
forming a new mentoring program through his church, reaching
out to at-risk elementary students in his city.

*What about you? What's your next step?*

The well-being of life on earth starts with God. It starts with God
and extends *to* you . . . then *through* you. The world is broken, Jesus
came to heal it, and he summons and shapes you to join him in his
work. You matter. Your life counts.

The world needs your presence, your voice, your work. The
world needs who you are in Jesus, and what you bring through
Jesus. Your roommates need you. Your family needs you. Your co-
workers need you. Your city needs you. Your neighborhood needs
you. Your faith community needs you. Your parents need you.

Where you live and serve and play needs you. The cubicle, garage,
classroom or hospital. The athletic field, gym, restaurant, kitchen

or design studio. The library, operating base, counseling office, store, farm, vineyard, campus or church. The pub, body shop, toolshed, factory, dealership, courtroom, cannery or studio. The police force, Capitol Hill or Wall Street.

You get the picture. Your place needs you to walk and work and lead with Jesus—for the life of that place and of those people. They need you to live the summons to relationship, partnership and leadership with Jesus for the life of the world.

God is calling.

What story will we one day tell about you?

*What's your next step?*

# DISCUSSION GUIDE

This guide is in four parts, one for each section of the book. It is designed to be used in four meetings of 60-90 minutes each.

## Part One: Summoned

1. When have you known someone to experience a "wake up call" from God?

2. In what ways have you seen someone living God's summons to relationship, partnership or leadership?

3. What do you think the author means by leading with Jesus "for the life of the world" (p. 28)?

4. The author describes five ways that God can summon someone (pp. 29-31). Talk about your experience with one or more of these ways.

5. Describe a time when you surrendered to God's summons.

6. Talk about what you think keeps people from surrendering to God.

7. If you were to take one step this week toward more fully discovering or living out God's summons to you, what would that step be?

## Part Two: Shaped

1. What do you think of when you hear the word "shaped"?

2. Talk about a recent experience in which God shaped your character.

3. In addition to forgiveness, the author discusses four strategies we can use to strengthen our relationships (pp. 65-68). What do you make of these strategies?

4. Comment on a time when you dealt with baggage in your life.

5. When do you typically find it difficult to submit to authority figures in your life?

6. Talk about a time when someone helped you identify a blind spot.

7. Talk about a transition you've been through and how God used it to shape your life.

8. If you were to say "yes" this week to one area that God wants to shape in your life, what would that area be?

9. What step would you be willing to take in that area?

## Part Three: Sent

1. Describe a time when you were sent by someone on an errand or assignment.

2. The author discusses four ways that God speaks to us and guides us (pp. 115-17). Through which of these four do you find God most often speaking to you?

3. Discuss a recent example of God speaking to you about a situation in which you were asking for direction.

4. How have you helped people find meaning in something you've led?

5. Talk about a time when you found it necessary to cry out to God for help.

6. The author identifies six ways to connect with God, beginning on page 140. Which of these ways could be helpful for your fellowship with God?

7. If you were to fight for something in your life this week, what would you fight for?

8. The author speaks of "Flipping Culture the Bird" (p. 171) in its treatment of women. If you were to do that this week, what would it look like?

## Part Four: Supported

1. We can go far in life when we have others to support us. Talk about a time when you witnessed someone enjoying the support of a group of friends or colleagues.

2. The author discusses seven types of mentors in chapter fifteen. Which of these types have you had in your life?

3. Which type do you need now?

4. Talk about a time when you've mentored someone else.

5. Which type of mentor were you during that time?

6. What's been your experience with connecting with other men in your life?

7. If you were to convene a group of men who would follow Jesus together, what would you want group meetings to include?

8. The author discusses what Jesus can do when a group of men gather to meet with him (page 196, "Jesus and Our Fire Pit Groups"). What do you make of what he says Jesus can do?

9. What could you offer someone this week who needs your support?

# ACKNOWLEDGMENTS

I've written *Summoned* to pass on lessons I've learned about God's call; about how God shapes leaders, especially their character formation; about stepping out to lead; and about connecting with others who can help us along the path. If I have anything to say about these topics, it's because of those in my life like Don Price, Wendell Geist, Don Burchfield and the men of Alpha Gamma Chi who gave me my first shots at learning to lead. It's also because of Bobby Clinton, Dan Reeves, Tom Paterson and Terry Walling, who taught me how God shapes leaders and coaches us on life direction.

The tipping point for writing occurred when Trey Miller and I were sorting out some of his stuff, and he turned the conversation to encourage me. (Trey had been one of the guys in my *Men Following Jesus* group at the University of Virginia.) He said something like this: "Have you ever thought about writing a book, Daniel? What if you wrote a book for me and Hall, Joe, Reilly, Mark and David [the other guys in the group]? Put into writing the stuff you've been telling us and guys like us. A book that will make us cry. A book that will give us your voice. Nobody gets honest with us like you do. Nobody's writing about their hardships and failures. Write a book like that."

Men from our *Men Following Jesus* groups at the University of Virginia and in Knoxville read drafts of early sections, as did Tyler Crowley, Micah Voraritskul, Jay Temple, Craig Chong, John Platillero, Colonel Wade, Jim Lewis, Mike Lewis, Danny Bullington,

Terry Walling, Steve Rankin, Kindra Greene, Kai Ryan, Nicole Unice, Gary Ray and my wife, Lainie.

David Wallace kept me tall in the saddle. Austin Church kept telling me I could write. Lainie and our team of prayer partners interceded for me. Greg Johnson at WordServe Literary Group did his best to keep me patient throughout the process and kept knocking on doors. Carrie Boren at the Episcopal Diocese of Dallas introduced me to Al Hsu at InterVarsity Press. Al and his team encouraged me and refined my raw material. For the contributions of each of these comrades (and any I may have overlooked), I am deeply grateful.

# NOTES

## Chapter 1: Wake-up Call

[1]*Oxford Dictionaries, s.v.* "*summon,*" accessed March 10, 2013, www
.oxforddictionaries.com/us/definition/american_english/summon?
q=summon.

[2]Richard A. Muller, *Dictionary of Latin and Greek Theological Terms:
Drawn Principally from Protestant Scholastic Theology* (Grand Rapids:
Baker Books, 1985), p. 329.

[3]See also Gordon T. Smith's *Courage and Calling* (Downers Grove, IL: Inter-
Varsity Press, 1999) for his understanding of the three parts of God's call.

[4]See chapter 3 for more on making peace with it.

[5]Ken Blanchard and Phil Hodges, *Lead Like Jesus* (Nashville: Thomas
Nelson, 2006), p. 4.

[6]Robert Greenleaf, *Servant Leadership* (Mahwah, NJ: Paulist Press,
1977).

[7]Dallas Willard, *The Divine Conspiracy* (New York: Harper Collins, 1998).

[8]J. Robert Clinton, *Strategic Concepts* (Altadena, CA: Barnabas Resources,
2005), pp. 73-82.

[9]Elmer Towns, *Getting a Church Started* (Lynchburg, VA: Church Growth
Institute, 1984), p. 28.

[10]The mentor was Tom Paterson, who writes about the life-direction
process he pioneered in his *Living the Life You Were Meant to Live* (Nashville: Thomas Nelson, 1998).

[11]Dan Allender, *To Be Told* (Colorado Springs, CO: WaterBrook, 2005),
p. 103. Along a similar line of thought, see Parker Palmer, *Let Your Life
Speak* (San Francisco: John Wiley & Sons, 2000).

[12]See "Our founder Chuck Colson," Prison Fellowship, www.prison
fellowship.org/about/.

[13]See www.newyorker.com/reporting/2009/01/19/090119fa_fact_power.

[14]Craig Dunham and Doug Severn, *TwentySomeone: Finding Yourself in a Decade of Transition* (Colorado Springs, CO: WaterBrook, 2003), p. 15. Emphasis original.

[15]A timeline often helps people understand and tell their story. You can access a free version at www.leaderbreakthru.com/sovereign-perspective /post-it-note-timeline.php.

## Chapter 2: Surrender

[1]Brent Curtis and John Eldredge, *The Sacred Romance* (Nashville: Thomas Nelson, 1997), p. 76.

[2]J. Robert Clinton, *Leadership Emergence Theory* (Altadena, CA: Barnabas Resources, 1989), p. 146. For a more popularized version of his work, see *The Making of a Leader: Recognizing the Lessons and Stages of Leadership Development*, 2nd ed. (Colorado Springs, CO: NavPress, 2012).

[3]Image created by Tom Paterson, Copyright © 2014, Paterson Center. Used by permission.

[4]Ibid., p. 94.

## Chapter 3: Finding *It*

[1]Jeffrey Jensen Arnett, *Emerging Adulthood: The Winding Road from the Late Teens through the Twenties* (New York: Oxford University Press, 2004).

[2]The Clark University Poll of Emerging Adults, December 2012, p. 14. See www.clarku.edu/clark-poll-emerging-adults/

[3]Arnett, *Emerging Adulthood*, p. 146.

[4]Walter Ciszek, *He Leadeth Me* (San Francisco: Ignatius Press, 1995), pp. 102-103. I first learned of Father Ciszek through Chris Lowney's *Heroic Living* (Chicago: Loyola Press, 2009), pp. 117-19.

[5]Macrina Wiederkehr, *Seven Sacred Pauses* (Notre Dame: Sorin Books, 2008), p. 24.

[6]Craig Dunham and Doug Serven, *TwentySomeone: Finding Yourself in a Decade of Transition.* (Colorado Springs, CO: WaterBrook), 2003, p. 95. Italics original.

[7]Jeffrey Jensen Arnett, "The Psychology of Emerging Adulthood: What Is Known, and What Remains to Be Known," in *Emerging Adults in America: Coming of Age in the 21st Century,* eds. Jeffrey Jensen Arnett and Jennifer Lynn Tanner (Washington, DC: American Psychological Association, 2006), p. 319.

[8]Mark Banschick, "Failure to Launch—Male and Stuck at Home," *The Intelligent Divorce (blog)*, Psychology Today, October 12, 2012, www .psychologytoday.com/blog/the-intelligent-divorce/201210/failure-launch-male-and-stuck-home.

[9]Meg Jay, *The Defining Decade: Why Your Twenties Matter—and How to Make the Most of Them Now* (New York: Hatchette Book Group, 2012), pp. 141-42.

[10]Dunham and Serven, *TwentySomeone*, p. 7.

## Chapter 4: Porn

[1]What do you fantasize about? Men, women or both? Same-sex relationships? Something else? Where does that fantasizing take you?

[2]J. Robert Clinton coined the term "integrity check" in his *Leadership Emergence Theory* (Altadena, CA: Barnabas Resources, 1989), pp. 90-91.

[3]Ibid., pp. 129-32.

[4]David L. Fleming, *What Is Ignatian Spirituality?* (Chicago: Loyola Press, 2008), pp. 7-11.

[5]The "purity lesson" is one of forty-one major leadership lessons in the Bible. It states that "leaders must personally learn of and respond to the holiness of God in order to have effective ministry." J. Robert Clinton and Daniel Allen, *Nehemiah: Focused Leaders* (Altadena, CA: Barnabas Resources), p. 133.

[6]See Bill Struthers, *Wired for Intimacy: How Pornography Hijacks the Male Brain* (Downers Grove, IL: InterVarsity Press, 2009), chap. 7.

## Chapter 5: Relationships

[1]Lewis Smedes was my ethics professor in seminary. I was taking his course at the time, and his book on forgiveness was a huge help: *Forgive & Forget: Healing the Hurts We Don't Deserve* (New York: HarperCollins, 1996).

[2]Ibid., chap. 5.

[3]Stephen R. Covey, *The Seven Habits of Highly Effective People* (New York: Simon & Schuster, 1989), pp. 235-60.

## Chapter 6: Baggage

[1]Brené Brown, *The Gifts of Imperfection* (Center City, MN: Hazelden, 2010), p. 41.

[2]Daniel Siegel, *Mindsight: The New Science of Personal Transformation* (New York: Bantam, 2011), pp. 195-96.

[3]Brent Curtis and John Eldredge, *The Sacred Romance* (Nashville: Thomas Nelson, 1997), chap. 3.

## Chapter 7: Bosses

[1]I'm not referring here to sexual, emotional or physical abuse at the hands of authority figures.

[2]J. Robert Clinton, *Leadership Emergence Theory* (Altadena, CA: Barnabas Resources, 1989), pp. 172-73.

[3]Michael Hyatt, "What If You Work for a Bad Leader?" *Michael Hyatt* (blog), November 25, 2013, http://michaelhyatt.com/what-if-you-work-for-a-bad-leader.html.

[4]Margie Warrell, "How to Handle a Bad Boss," *Forbes*, January 20, 2014, www.forbes.com/sites/margiewarrell/2014/01/20/6-strategies-to-hanhandldling-a-bad-boss/.

[5]Hyatt, "What If You Work for a Bad Leader?"

[6]Michael Hyatt, "How to Coach Your Boss" *Michael Hyatt* (blog), August 7, 2013, http://michaelhyatt.com/061-how-to-coach-your-boss-podcast.html.

[7]Warrell, "How to Handle a Bad Boss."

[8]Parker J. Palmer, *Leading from Within: Reflections on Spirituality and Leadership* (Washington, DC: The Servant Leadership School, 1990), pp. 7.

## Chapter 8: Blind Spots

[1]For further information, go to "The Johari Window," Primary Goals, OD Resources, www.primarygoals.org/models/johari-window/.

[2]Edgar H. Schein, *Organizational Culture and Leadership* (San Francisco: Jossey-Bass Publishers, 1992).

[3]J. Robert Clinton, *Leadership Emergence Theory* (Altadena, CA: Barnabas Resources, 1989), pp. 174-75.

[4]From Schein, chap. 2.

## Chapter 9: Lost in Transition

[1]J. Robert Clinton, *Leadership Emergence Theory* (Altadena, CA: Barnabas Resources, 1989), pp. 305-8 for transitions (also called boundaries); p. 274 for isolation. See Terry Walling's *Stuck! Navigating the Transitions of Life and Leadership* (Orlando, FL: ChurchSmart Resources, 2008) for a book-length treatment of three major transitions in leaders' lives.

[2]Craig Dunham and Doug Serven, *TwentySomeone: Finding Yourself in a*

*Decade of Transition* (Colorago Springs, CO: WaterBrook, 2003), p. 6.

[3]Alexandra Robbins and Abby Wilner, *Quarterlife Crisis* (New York: Jeremy P. Tarcher/Putnam, 2001).

[4]Jeffrey Jensen Arnett, *Emerging Adulthood: The Winding Road from the Late Teens through the Twenties* (New York: Oxford University Press, 2004), pp. 3-4.

[5]Ibid., p. 3.

[6]Ibid., p. 8.

[7]J. Robert Clinton, *Leadership Emergence Theory* (Altadena, CA: Barnabas Resources, 1989), pp. 293-96. Used by permission.

[8]Ibid., pp. 274-75. For a more extended and personal look at isolation, see Shelley Trebesch, *Isolation: A Place of Transformation in the Life of a Leader* (Altadena, CA: Barnabas Resources, 1997).

[9]J. Robert Clinton, *The Making of a Leader* (Colorado Springs, CO: NavPress, 2012), p. 141. Used by permission.

## Chapter 10: Getting Direction

[1]J. Robert Clinton, *Leadership Emergence Theory* (Altadena, CA: Barnabas Resources, 1989), pp. 133, 182.

[2]See Bobby Clinton's paper, "Various Inputs on Guidance" (Altadena, CA: Barnabas Resources, 2010). For more on recognizing God's voice, dive into Dallas Willard's *Hearing God: Developing a Conversational Relationship with God* (Downers Grove, IL: InterVarsity Press, 1999).

[3]Churches within the Anglican Communion generally speak of two dominical sacraments: Baptism and the Holy Eucharist. Roman Catholic and Orthodox churches identify seven sacraments.

## Chapter 11: Making Meaning

[1]This was 1983, *twenty-six years* before Simon Sinek's popular TED talk on the power of why, "How Great Leaders Inspire Action," TED, www.ted .com/talks/simon_sinek_how_great_leaders_inspire_action.html.

[2]John White, *Excellence in Leadership* (Downers Grove, IL: InterVarsity Press, 1986), p. 11.

[3]Rick Warren, "Leadership Lifter—Principles of Leadership: Meditation and Relaxation," PurposeDriven Small Group Network, May 29, 2010, http://pdsgn.wordpress.com/category/leadership-lifters-by-rick-warren/.

[4]In addition to *Mindsight* by Daniel J. Siegel (New York: Random

House, 2010), see the white paper by Nick Petrie, "Wake Up! The Surprising Truth About What Drives Stress and How Leaders Build Resilience" (Greensboro, NC: Center for Creative Leadership, 2013), accessed at www.ccl.org/leadership/pdf/research/WakeUp.pdf.

[5]Rick Warren, *God's Power to Change Your Life* (Grand Rapids: Zondervan, 2006) p. 202.

[6]Stephen Covey calls this "sharpening your saw." See his comments on the production/production capacity concept and the seventh habit in his *The Seven Habits of Highly Effective People* (Simon & Schuster, 2013).

## Chapter 12: Plugging In

[1]J. Robert Clinton and Daniel Allen, *Nehemiah: Focused Leaders* (Altadena, CA: Barnabas Resources), p. 82.

[2]John Eldredge, *Wild at Heart: Discovering the Secret of a Man's Soul* (Nashville: Thomas Nelson, 2001), p. 171 (italics his).

[3]James Bryan Smith, *Hidden in Christ* (Downers Grove, IL: InterVarsity Press, 2013), p. 133.

[4]Chester Michael and Marie Norrisey explore the connection between prayer and the Myers-Briggs framework in their book *Prayer and Temperament* (Charlottesville, VA: The Open Door Publishers, 1991).

[5]Myra Perrine, *What's Your God Language?* (Carol Stream, IL: Tyndale House, 2007), chap. 12.

## Chapter 13: Fighting Back

[1]J. Robert Clinton, *Leadership Emergence Theory* (Altadena, CA: Barnabas Resources, 1989), pp. 238-39.

[2]C. S. Lewis, *The Screwtape Letters* (New York: HarperCollins Edition, 2001), preface.

[3]John Eldredge, *Wild at Heart: Discovering the Secret of a Man's Soul* (Nashville: Thomas Nelson, 2001), p. 162.

[4]Keith Beasley-Topliffe, ed., *Seeking a Purer Christian Life: Sayings and Stories of the Desert Fathers and Mothers* (Nashville: Upper Room Books, 2000), p. 19.

[5]Ibid., p. 20.

[6]Ibid., p. 22.

## Chapter 14: Teaming Up

[1]Ellen F. Davis, *Getting Involved with God: Rediscovering the Old Tes-

*tament* (Lanham, MD: Rowman & Littlefield Publishers, 2001), p. 71. See especially her thoughts on the Song of Songs 5:10–7:11 and how it sounds a reversal of Genesis 3:16 (p. 72).

[2]Tom Wright, *Luke for Everyone* (Louisville, KY: Westminster John Knox Press, 2001), pp. 130-31.

[3]Part of my problem with the position that opposes women ministering in the church is that, to make its case, it singles out a few verses of Scripture that seem to contradict the overarching posture of Jesus toward women and the occasions of men and women working together in ministry. For a fuller treatment of the issues, see Scot McKnight, *The Blue Parakeet: Rethinking How You Read the Bible* (Grand Rapids: Zondervan, 2008); Gordon D. Fee, *1 and 2 Timothy, Titus* (Peabody, MA: Hendrickson Publishers, 1988), pp. 70-77; and N. T. Wright, "Women's Service in the Church: The Biblical Basis," conference paper presented at the symposium Men, Women and the Church, St John's College, Durham, UK, September 4, 2004, accessed at http://ntwrightpage.com/Wright_Women_Service_Church.htm.

[4]Holly Moore, "From Awkward to Authentic: Four Ways Men Can Lead Women Well," *Growing Leaders*, March 25, 2014, http://growingleaders.com/blog/awkward-authentic-four-ways-men-can-lead-women-well/.

[5]John Gerzema, "Girl Power," *Spirit Magazine*, May 2013, p. 44.

[6]"New Zealand Teen Rape Club Is the Worst Thing You'll Read about Today," Jezebel, November 5, 2013, http://jezebel.com/new-zealand-teen-rape-club-is-the-worst-thing-youll-re-1458798760.

[7]Juliet Macur and Nate Schweber, "Rape Case Unfolds on Web and Splits City," New York Times online, December 16, 2012, www.nytimes.com/2012/12/17/sports/high-school-football-rape-case-unfolds-online-and-divides-steubenville-ohio.html?pagewanted=all&_r=0.

[8]You can read about the incident at www.thedailybeast.com/articles/2012/07/11/why-daniel-tosh-s-rape-joke-at-the-laugh-factory-wasn-t-funny.html.

[9]Audrey Gill, "Top 10 Tips for Men to Avoid Committing Rape," *The Daily Campus*, November 11, 2013, p. 4. To their credit, managing editor W. Tucker Keene and contributing writer Ruby Kim penned articles titled "The Dangers of Hook-Up Culture" and "Yes Means Yes: A Culture Of Consent," respectively.

[10]www.secondlifechattanooga.org.

## Chapter 15: Mentors

[1]Paul D. Stanley and J. Robert Clinton, *Connecting: The Mentoring Relationships You Need to Succeed in Life* (Colorado Springs, CO: NavPress, 1992) p. 33.

[2]Ibid., pp. 28-29.

[3]Discipleship Cycle Card, InterVarsity Christian Fellowship, 2014.

## Chapter 16: Other Men

[1]What I say about this John 21 passage is not the standard way in which this chapter has been interpreted. What I'm trying to do is apply what John says about *Jesus* to the groups we lead, not find in these verses justification for having men's meetings.

[2]Parker Palmer's observations about the Quaker tradition's way of helping one another with our inner work are instructive: "They come together with them in a way that is supportive but not invasive, that asks a lot of questions but never renders judgment or gives advice. They come together in a way that respects the mystery of the human heart, but that still allows people to challenge and stretch one another in that work." Parker J. Palmer, *Leading from Within: Reflections on Spirituality and Leadership* (Washington, DC: The Servant Leadership School, 1990), p. 19.

# ABOUT THE AUTHOR

Daniel Allen (DMin, Fuller Theological Seminary) is a leadership coach, pathfinder, teacher and author. For more than two decades, he has helped college students and young adults discern their gifts and identify the unique ways that God is calling them to lead lives of influence. Daniel currently works with the Episcopal Diocese of Dallas to catalyze leadership formation and discipleship initiatives on nearby college campuses. When Daniel isn't working with young adult leaders, the self-proclaimed "plodder" is usually training for a half or full marathon. Though he and his wife Lainie live near the campus of Southern Methodist University, Daniel remains faithful to his beloved Carolina Tar Heels.

www.summonedbook.com

www.danielallenjr.com